DYING LIGHT

AN INVESTIGATION INTO NEAR-DEATH EXPERIENCES

JASON HEWLETT

PETER RENN

BEYOND THE FRAY

Publishing

ISBN 13: 978-1-954528-43-7

Beyond The Fray Publishing, a division of Beyond The Fray, LLC, San Diego, CA
www.beyondthefraypublishing.com

BEYOND THE FRAY

Publishing

CONTENTS_

CHAPTER ONE_
WHY WRITE A BOOK ABOUT DEATH?

When Peter and I sat down to research and interview paranormal investigators and cryptozoologists for our second book, *I Want to Believe: An Investigators' Archive*, we thought a third book would continue along the paranormal path with a focus on residential investigations.

Then we interviewed friend and colleague Angela Artuso, who shared with us a story about a near-death experience that stunned Peter and me. The experience, which you will read later in this book, was so powerful and compelling it sparked in us a desire to look deeper into the phenomenon and the lifelong impact it has on the experiencer.

Peter had a near-death experience prior to his liver transplant. We made mention of that in our first book, *I Want to Believe: One Man's Journey into the Paranormal*, and he describes the event and how it changed him later in this volume (yup, I'm a tease). So where does that leave yours truly?

I've never had a near-death experience, at least not in the same way as those being reported by four to fifteen percent of the population per year. These reports come from adults, children, physicians... you name it. It's a phenomenon that crosses all genders, professions, and ethnicities.

I am, however, no stranger to death. While my interest in the paranormal and what happens to us when we die was sparked early in life, I didn't begin to take a hard look at it until my father passed away when I was nineteen. He was fifty-six and had, up until the moment of his death, seemed perfectly healthy. He'd given up smoking when I was five, exercised regularly, and watched his diet, including drinking very little alcohol. In essence, he did everything you were supposed to do to encourage a long and happy life.

But on September 24, 1991, he fell ill while on a job site (he was a building contractor and architect). His brother and business partner decided the best course of action would be to drive my father to the hospital, as there didn't seem to be anything physically wrong with him. Half-way during the ten-minute drive to the hospital, my father said, "I think everything is going to be okay. I feel better." His brother decided to keep going, as they were minutes away from the emergency room doors.

A block out, with the hospital in clear view of their approaching truck, my dad slumped over in his seat dead.

A post mortem determined Dad had died from a heart attack caused by an erratic heart rate he'd had since birth, which hadn't been previously diagnosed. The short story was it didn't matter how well he took care of himself, his number was up, and that was it.

Aside from being the most traumatic event of my young life, Dad's death and the circumstances surrounding it changed the way I looked at the world. If doing all the right things when it came to maintaining good health and prolonging your life didn't work, then what was the point? It also spurred a curiosity in what happens to us when we die. Where do we go? Does life continue after death?

I didn't take action on those questions until 2003, when I was in my first year of journalism school. I'd basically free-floated through life up to that point, bouncing from one idea of who or what I was and what I wanted to be to another. I'd had a series of failed relationships, completed a degree in film studies, and done some travelling. I liked to write and figured journalism was my best bet for getting paid to do it, so I jumped on that bandwagon.

Although I'd never conducted a formal paranormal investigation – outside of a few drunken Ouija board sessions – I had maintained an interest in the subject. One of the classes I enrolled in during that first year of journalism studies was a magazine writing class where we had a whole semester to research and write an article for the magazine of our choosing. I loved reading the Fortean Times, an esteemed publication on the paranormal out of the United Kingdom, and decided to write an article with the intention of submitting it at the end of the school year.

What transpired was my first serious stab at a paranormal investigation, and my first attempt at answering the question of what happens when we die. There's a former tuberculosis clinic and mental institution in my home town called Tranquille Sanitarium, which has a storied history of hauntings and weird encounters. I managed to find someone who'd had such an encounter and recruited a psychic, a skeptic, and a cameraman to join me on an overnight investigation. Being friends with the caretaker opened the doors on a cold February night, and we went in hoping to find something.

We didn't, but we had a really good time, and I got an A on the article. For the record, I never submitted it to Fortean Times.

The experience did start a series of investigations, often solo ones at Tranquille. I didn't know what I was doing, and made a lot of mistakes, but the adventures did result in one of the most frightening encounters I've had with the paranormal, and one that cemented in me an understanding that there's more to life than what we see on the surface.

My friend and psychic Donna and I were exploring the tunnels beneath Tranquille. It snows a lot where I live in Western Canada, so a tunnel system was created between all the asylum's buildings to move patients and supplies from building to building during the heavier winters. The tunnels are unlit, vast, and are rumoured – like the rest of the former sanitarium – to be haunted.

We spent a good hour wandering the tunnels with flashlights in hand, and came up a flight of stairs into what was once the laundry facility. It was getting late, and we figured it was time to return to the car and head home. The debate began: do we go back to the vehicle above ground, or take the tunnels in hope of having a spooky encounter? We opted for the tunnels.

I turned and grabbed the handle of the door we'd just passed through. I pulled it open, and the door obeyed for a few feet before something grabbed hold of the door and pulled it shut, with enough force that I was hauled off my feet and slammed into it!

There was no draft or air flow that could've caused the door to do that. And I'm not a small man, carrying almost one hundred and ninety pounds on my six-foot-one frame.

Donna screamed and ran. I admit, I wasn't far behind her.

The experience altered my enthusiasm for the paranormal. Before, I was just interested in it on the level of it being a lark. I'd had weird, and at times creepy, experiences before but this was the first time I was physically affected by it. It was terrifying!

At about the same time, I began my career in journalism as a crime reporter for the local daily newspaper. I quieted my enthusiasm for the supernatural, as I quickly learned any expression of interest in the subject could kill my credibility as a reporter, although my interest never waned. However, I became very intimate with the subject of death.

There's a saying in news, "If it bleeds, it leads." My job found me at every terrible thing that happened in my home town and the surrounding region. Murders, auto accidents, fires – you name it, I was in the thick of it. At first, it was exhilarating. I rode with firefighters and police officers, and even spent time with the military flying in gunships. All of this was done on a daily deadline, and the adrenalin rush was unlike anything I'd experienced before.

Something changed after a couple of years of this. I'd lost track of the number of dead bodies I'd seen, this includes watching a woman burn to death in a car wreck. I'd stood meters from two children who'd died in a cabin fire, and walked through places where people had been murdered. Each time I felt the trauma that had occurred, and each time I felt like I lost a part of myself.

I remember getting called to the local beach because a

man had walked into the river intent on drowning himself, and the fire department was called to rescue him. I'd already been to the scene of a fatal accident that week, and stood on the grass watching firefighters revive this man. In my head I kept screaming, "Don't you die, you selfish bastard. Don't you die."

He died in the back of an ambulance on the way to the hospital.

We didn't make a habit of writing about suicides unless they were done in public, and one such death haunts me some fifteen years later. A women stood on the train tracks in a suburban neighborhood, a cross in hand, and waited for a train to run her over. The place she picked to do this was wide open, so the conductor had plenty of time to slow the train, which takes a good mile or two to go from full speed to full stop.

By the time the train reached her, it rolled right over top of her, pulling her into the wheels. I remember standing back, watching firefighters try to pry her from beneath the train. A cop I knew well was there, and he walked over to me, tears in his eyes. This guy was a stereotypical tough guy, so his tears startled me.

"What's going on?" I asked.

He told me the woman's limbs were wrapped up in the wheels, and the firefighters were having a hard time getting her untangled. "The thing is," he continued, "she's still alive. And she's not making a sound."

She too died on the way to the hospital.

Years later I learned when someone experiences trauma, as I had with the passing of my father, a part of the brain is damaged and never heals. The "scar," for lack of a better word, just gets bigger. By the time a psychiatrist diagnosed me with post traumatic stress disorder, my scar was described as a super-highway. Having not resolved the grief of my father's death, I was the worst possible candidate for a crime reporter.

Surprisingly, it wasn't my career as a crime reporter that drove me to counselling. My son was born months earlier with congenital hypothyroidism, which we discovered ten days after he was born. This meant he will always take a thyroid pill in order for his body to function properly. The first few months were terrifying, as he never put on weight no matter how much food he ate. He nearly died. I can still remember the overwhelming sense of relief when the doctor told my wife and me our boy had actually gained a couple of pounds.

My personal traumas mixed with a decade of vicariously experiencing every kind of horrible and untimely death left me questioning not only the point of life, but what happens when we die. There was a time I was terrified of the idea, so much so I spent a month convinced I wouldn't wake up if I fell asleep. Many a night I'd be on the cusp of sleep, my eyes heavy and ready to close, when

I'd bolt awake afraid it would be for the last time. It felt like I was losing my mind!

Fortunately, those days passed thanks to the support of my wife, close friends, and counsellor. And, once the newspaper closed its doors in 2014, I started to put those vicarious traumas behind me and heal thanks to a new career in employment counselling. I met a whole new group of people, most with a positive outlook on life, and put my reporter skills to good use helping people find work. Although I eventually left that job, I credit it and the people I met with helping turn my world view around and work through a lot of my career-related grief.

During this time, I met Peter Renn and joined the Vancouver Paranormal Society. Many of these adventures were chronicled in our first book, *I Want to Believe: One Man's Journey into the Paranormal*. For the first time in my life I was able to take a good, hard and professional – well, as close to professional given the line of work – look at paranormal investigations. Although nothing we've found to date would hold up in a court of law, which Shawn Knippelberg, co-producer and composer for our web series *We Want to Believe*, says is the requirement for good, hard evidence, we've encountered much to validate my experience in the tunnels of Tranquille all those years ago.

Over the years Peter, our team, and I have amassed several EVPs (electronic voice phenomena) that suggest an unseen intelligence exists around us and can even interact with us given the right line of questioning. We've captured photographs of apparitions at historical locations, seen doors close by themselves and toys fly off shelves, and recorded video of a possible shadow figure using our laser grid, a device that casts an array of lights across a room in a grid-like pattern. The theory is even something unseen can block out the lasers if it crosses in front of the beams. That's exactly what happened in this case, and we caught it on camera!

These experiences have left me with no doubt in my mind that life doesn't stop when we die. Where do we go though? Is there a heaven and hell? Are we born again into another life, hence reincarnation? Or do we continue on as another version of ourselves in a different universe, hence the multiverse concept mainstream science is taking serious a look at.

As I mentioned at the beginning of this chapter, I've not had a near-death experience like Peter or the people whose stories we chronicle in this book. But I did have an unexplainable experience that rattled me to my core and opened my mind to what possibly happens when we die.

My wife and son had gone to bed, and I'd stayed up to watch a movie and enjoy a couple of beers. I went outside to get some air and, given it was a cold November night in 2018, quickly became chilled. So I went back inside and got ready for bed. However, the chill never left me. In fact, I felt colder and colder and the shakes got worse, continuing after I crawled into bed. For the first time in years I was convinced I would die if I went to sleep.

Then I heard a voice in my head tell me it was time to choose where I want to go next. A number of possibilities were opened to me: I could go to a life where Dad hadn't died, where I'd married a woman who wasn't my wife, and on and on into what felt like an infinite number of possibilities... but if I chose one of them, I would leave behind this life forever.

My body shook uncontrollably, and my terrified mind raced. But over and over in my head I repeated the phrase, "I love my wife and son and the life we have!" I managed to reach out for my wife, who woke up by now given how upset I'd become. She held me and was shocked by how cold my body had become. She said it felt like I'd been outside with no clothes on for hours.

I finally calmed down, and the feeling of dread left. My body warmed up, and I fell asleep in her arms. Morning came. It was my son's seventh birthday. I was very apologetic to my wife for waking her, but she shrugged it off and promised she wasn't going anywhere.

I've never forgotten the offer the voice made me: that I could go anywhere and live any life as long as I was willing to leave this one behind.

Whatever caused that experience to happen, I've seen life and death differently since. Being able to interview the people for this book and do the research to better understand the near-death experience has been a healing process of sorts for myself. I'm not sure I believe everything Peter and I heard during the writing of this book, but I know better than to discount something simply because I didn't experience it.

I hope you enjoy reading this book as much as we enjoyed researching and writing it.

CHAPTER TWO_
ON GRIEF AND TRAUMA

GIVEN SHE'S DEDICATED A GOOD PORTION OF HER LIFE to helping others through their grief and trauma, it should come as no surprise the journey started as a personal one for Jolene Lindsey.

Lindsey was seventeen when she lost her dad to suicide, a loss that's impossible to describe unless you've lost a loved one in such a traumatic fashion. Her dad's suicide so sidelined her with grief she even attempted to take her own life.

Fortunately, she wasn't able to pull herself out of that downward spiral. Instead, she transformed it into a wisdom, passion and power for helping others through their pain, taking the lessons she learned with her healing and applying them to her professional practice.

"That's a huge catalyst to why I am where I am now,"

says Lindsey, a registered social worker and grief, trauma and life transitions counsellor.

What she's also witnessed, working so closely with those who have lost loved ones, is a kind of "outside influence," which guides her work and leads those who are in need of help toward her.

Yes, she's talking about spirits.

"It's really neat. I've really come to embrace that," says Lindsey.

At first, Lindsey felt professionally conflicted for even considering a spiritual component to her work. As a social worker and counsellor, there's generally a heavy emphasis on psychology, sociology, and the workings of the mind. As with science, there's not a lot of acceptance when it comes to the concepts of ghosts and spirits, at least within the mainstream.

But these "nudgings" were frequent enough she couldn't ignore them. The subtle coincidences that led clients to her door, not to mention that she believes many of the homes she's lived in – and currently lives in – are cohabitated by ghosts.

Surprisingly, this spiritual energy made itself known during the COVID-19 pandemic, when Lindsey was forced to conduct the majority of her work with clients online. She says it started showing up everywhere, from her internet connection to "glitches" during video calls.

"I see way more of spirit energy and presence online than I ever did in person," she says.

Lindsey specializes in Eye Movement Desensitization and Reprocessing Therapy (EMDR). This is a form of psychotherapy in which the person being treated is asked to recall distressing images. The therapist then directs the patient in one type of bilateral stimulation, such as side-to-side rapid movements or hand tapping. It's believed effective because recalling distressing events is often less emotionally upsetting when one's attention is diverted, allowing the patient to be exposed to these memories and thoughts without having a strong psychological response.

I've been treated with EMDR, and found myself entering an almost trancelike state while working through past traumas in my personal and professional life. I can also say it was quite effective and helped me overcome many negative thoughts, feelings and behaviours.

What Lindsey found while working online is the screen would freeze or cut out at key moments during sessions, while she moved her hands or changed targets for the patient to focus on, she says. And these pixelations in the video occur while the client was getting to the root cause of the trauma that brought him or her to Lindsey's practice.

She says these interferences are the spirits of loved ones trying to make contact with her clients during therapy sessions, often acting as "exclamation points" and guides to the work being done.

"I would start to notice things like that. Electronically, there was a lot of interference in the beginning. Now I kind of work with them and say, 'You gotta let us talk. You can present yourself, and make yourself known, but you can't interfere with the actual healing process,'" she says.

More than one of Lindsey's clients has had a near-death experience, and several have found themselves in palliative care, dying of cancer or about to transition into death. The majority of her work, though, is with people who have lost loved ones and are longing to make that connection with them on the other side and have that sense of healing.

"That really changes the grieving process, when they have that connection with their loved one on the other side," she says.

Given her personal and professional encounters with death, there's similar characteristics to these death and near-death experiences. A lot of the work she does is through the lens of trauma and how it allows, or prevents, people to move forward in their lives.

For one, whether the person has been close to death, or actually died for a time, his or her world view drastically changes, says Lindsey. They live their lives differently, and literally see life in a whole new way.

"They start to consciously pay attention to life differently," she says.

Typically, people either view the world through a dark lens, seeing hazards everywhere, or they see things in a positive way, realizing life's little coincidences aren't really coincidences at all, but part of some larger plan.

Quite often, the initial world view is quite dark, says Lindsey. People get caught up in self-defeating behaviour driven by hypervigilance. When something life-altering and traumatic happens, the desire is to prevent something like this from happening again, hence the survivor is on the lookout for potential danger so he or she can avoid them and help their loved ones do the same.

In Lindsey's case, she was easygoing and laid back prior to her dad's suicide and her own attempt. Afterwards, there was a powerful anxiety within her to control life and prevent another unexpected tragedy from happening.

"I always had that driving force of my dad's death propelling me forward – kind of like that beacon in the distance – but there was a shit show of things to navigate between there and now," she says, adding she now views life through a positive and very spiritual lens.

"I think that people, no matter what, will face times of darkness. It is how we learn to heal, grow and transform within that which will set us free from its clutches. If you don't transform that pain, it'll take you down."

Depression, addiction, loss of a relationship or a career are just some of the ways remaining in those dark places can severely impact someone's life, she says. Some of Lindsey's clients have such massively complex trauma in their lives that the effects can take years of patient work to unravel and reprogram.

She shares details of one such person, a former soldier who suffered a massive accident while overseas in Germany that led to a near-death experience. Thirty years later he still woke up every October 15, the day of the accident, and smelled burning rubber and heard the screams of those who died. And even after all this time, he woke up roughly five nights a week sweating, and had to sit in his kitchen and smoke for three hours to calm down. Lindsey says he essentially relived the experience of being in battle.

"Then he goes up, changes his sheets, and tries to sleep again," she says. "And he would literally do that five nights a week."

Together, over the course of eight months, she's helped him heal enough he can now count the number of times that's happening on one hand, she says.

"How were you navigating life? Waking up and going to a job, living your life, navigating that almost every night?" Lindsey wonders. "It's wild what we're able to navigate in the dark depths. It always fascinates me. What is it that keeps people going? It doesn't have to be this hard though."

When it comes to near-death experiences, there are several commonalities experiencers say they encounter. The tunnel of light and the presence of another individual or groups of people who are present with the one who is dying. There's also an often overpowering desire to cross over from the world of the living to the other side. Setting her spiritual beliefs aside, Lindsey attempts to explain what this as a counsellor.

When people go into a fight-or-flight state, which a death experience would surely create, our nervous system becomes so hijacked we lose connection with the upper brain, which controls thinking, logic, reasoning and planning, says Lindsey. This leaves the individual with the primal brain in control, which is very basic and instinctual in its response. It may also trigger a dissociative trauma response that disconnects the person from the present.

"Ego, conditioned and socially constructed responses, and all of those things that shut down the sixth sense, the intuitive side of us. When all of that is halted, and we suddenly are able to see and receive without the judgment, the filters and the 'shoulds'," she says.

She likens this state to when we're children, who she believes are much more intuitive and in tune with the unseen world around us before that sensitivity is schooled and socialized out of us. Children, much like animals, visualize things with their conscious mind and not their logical mind.

"They don't question it, they just go with it," says Lindsey.

Lindsey hypothesizes this "openness" takes over during the flight-or-fight response of being near death, and potentially creates the near-death experience.

While fight or flight can empower people, most of the clients she sees in her line of work are frozen within their traumas. This creates a state of disassociation where a person's body is present, but the mind has "checked out," she says. This is particularly true among survivors of childhood trauma.

A common issue with highly spiritual and religious clients who rely solely on prayer and meditation as their healing is they can trigger dissociation, which puts them into a state outside of their body and prevents them from processing the root cause of their trauma in their physical body where it is stored, says Lindsey. A term for this can be "spiritual bypassing" by where the work isn't being integrated into the somatic storage of the trauma in the body and mind neurologically.

"I do a ton of work getting them back into their body because we can't heal what occurred when they are in that (dissociative) state. We need to heal it when they are in the physical state, where it is stored in the present body," she says.

"So part of me wonders if these near-death experiences are a part of a dissociative-type state."

Many near-death experiencers report hovering above their body or seeing themselves from a third-person viewpoint, which suggests the person is in a state of disassociation.

"I wonder if there's a massive state of disassociation where we're able to step out of our body and experience some of those other things?" Lindsey theorizes.

Indeed, there are a lot of parallels between what Lindsey presents and what survivors of near-death experiences describe. As she pointed out, there's the feeling of hovering above your body or viewing yourself in the third person, there's the tunnel of light, and there's the sense of another presence being nearby, either visible as a loved one who has already died or some unknown or even phantom being. Could these be the result of a person being in a fight-or-flight/dissociative state? Perhaps, at least from a counselling perspective, it is a possibility.

Putting her spiritual hat back on though, Lindsey believes it's also possible that those on the brink of death are communicating with whatever is on the other side. And if you're open-minded enough, that communication isn't limited to near-death experiences.

She cites the mysterious technical "glitches" she has experienced working with people online, or times she's posed a question to the universe and received an answer back. Lindsey also acknowledges this can be a hard concept for many people to follow.

"You could say 'Yeah, you were looking for the orange car, so you're going to see orange cars everywhere,'" says Lindsey. "But there's a feeling that accompanies that observation, and that feeling is what you can't dispute."

If science was able to capture those "a ha" moments that come with feeling in tune with the universe by hooking someone up to a heart monitor or recording the energy input that can occur during those moments – much like what she views on her computer screen during those virtual counselling sessions – those experiences might be validated, she says.

This works in much the same way as paranormal investigators who have personal experiences while exploring allegedly haunted locations. You hear a voice or see a shadow move, you know you saw it, but it wasn't picked up on audio or video and, therefore, isn't counted as evidence.

"The people who don't get it, won't get it, and that's okay because they just don't speak that language," says Lindsey.

"It's like you're gifted a direct phone line to the other side now, and if you don't have the fucking number, you don't have the conversation."

Given the subject matter of death, there are two belief systems: those who believe we transition to another side or state of being, and a growing number of atheists and agnostics who are convinced all existence ends when our brain and body dies. As a counsellor, Lindsey has a few thoughts on why there are still so many who hope for some kind of transcendence when this life ends.

Although she doesn't come from a religious upbringing, Lindsey was still convinced her dad wasn't simply "a rock in the ground" when he died. This belief was cemented when she became a full-fledged counsellor and worked with like-minded people. She says it quickly became clear that people can better resolve the pain of a loved one's death if there's a chance there's life beyond.

"People want to feel a connection, feel there's something more to life. Otherwise why? Why bother? What is the point? Why do we struggle, and why do we go through what we go through? What else is there?" she asks.

Those who do make a spiritual connection or encounter some kind of validation of their grief – in whatever form that might take – experience a sense of freedom and even permission to live that can be beautiful to witness, says Lindsey.

These people begin to live their lives differently, she says. They are more appreciative of what they have, they live with more intention, and the mind opens to a whole new level of awareness they didn't have before.

"I also think there's so much more that's offered to us in terms of the right connections being made. It's almost like you have this special little force working in your favor in a lot of ways. People will talk about that," Lindsey says.

While researching this book, Peter and I found our

interviewees either approached the subject of death and near-death experiences from either a spiritual or scientific perspective. To speak with Lindsey about the topic and find she was able to walk the fine line between both was refreshing. Lindsey is also a trained Holy Fire Reiki practitioner and has been mentored in mediumship, which has also given her an additional phone line to the other side to enhance her practice.

Lindsey says she's met doctors who at first explored the subject from a very medical and scientific methodology but, after having their own experience, began to see things in a more spiritual light. These about-faces are the most fascinating for her.

Perhaps it takes a personal encounter with death, either via the loss of a loved one or your own personal brush with the other side, to awaken that spiritual side of you?

This is something to keep in mind as we continue to explore this fascinating subject and speak with other experiencers and researchers on the topic.

CHAPTER THREE_

THE RESEARCHER

So we've covered some commonalities near-death experiencers have described when they awaken: the tunnel, the light, the other presence with them. We've also discussed both the psychological and spiritual possibilities behind these events.

As you can guess, this barely scratches the surface of what these people may be experiencing and how profound it can be.

Clearly there's a lot more ground to cover when exploring these death events, and in our quest to learn as much as possible, we turned to a variety of people for guidance and information. One of the most profound interviewees we encountered is Lynn Russell.

Russell is an author and researcher who worked with Jeffrey Long, a physician who's dedicated his life to

JASON HEWLETT & PETER RENN

exploring the near-death experience. While working with Long, she reviewed some two thousand five hundred near-death experiences, with people being dead for a matter of minutes up to as long as twenty-nine hours. Her findings tell us the near-death experience does have its commonalities but is also highly subjective, with the person's life experience playing a role in how the event plays out.

But why dedicate your life to exploring death? For Russell, it started as a child growing up with an atheist mother who told her when you die, you disappear.

"And that terrified me as a child," says Russell. "I was about eight or nine."

So she began searching for the truth, whether death was truly it, or if there was something more after we die. Her quest began with wanting to know about death, but quickly turned into a desire to know about the history of death and what it means. This led her to explore a variety of different religions and how they evolved into what they are today.

This was back before the spiritual movement of the 1960s and 1970s took place. When the movement started, Russell found herself drawn to it because she grew up without any religious influence. The concept of a holistic form of divinity that imbues the universe, including human beings themselves, was attractive to her, as was the idea each of us has a spiritual authority over ourselves. This was, of course, the New Age Movement.

During this time Russell was a family counsellor, an occupation she enjoyed for some thirty years. Once she retired, she found herself in a position to explore death in greater detail, and this led her to do research for Dr. Jeffrey Long and his first book on near-death experiences, *Evidence of the Afterlife: The Science of Near-Death Experiences*, which was published in 2010.

Even when her research for him was done, she kept studying the subject because she found it fascinating. She's since published her own book, *The Wonder of You: What the Near-Death Experience Tells You About Yourself.*

For her, it was messages that kept coming back with near-death experiencers that she found the most fascinating. She says these messages have a lot to say about our reality and what it's all about.

These messages were gleaned from the two thousand five hundred cases she's reviewed during her years of study. Although each of those incidents have similarities, no two near-death experiences are alike, says Russell.

All communication on the other side is done through telepathy and not talking, she says. This is a much faster way of communicating. Beings can also see in all directions at once, effectively making their vision a full three hundred and sixty degrees.

"They can understand multiple conversations without confusion. They can travel by just merely thinking about where they want to be," says Russell.

"They all, and this is almost universal, they all come back saying that they felt they were a part of everything. A part of the universe. And there was no separation between themselves and the physical universe."

Most, but not all, experiencers, continued to view themselves as physical beings on the other side, says Russell. They see a physical world around them. They see their loved ones and maybe even spirit guides. And, when they look at themselves, they see a physical body.

All this, however, is a construct of the mind because we are so used to being physical, she says.

Once on the other side, there is a powerful feeling of unconditional love and any past issues in a person's life – be it resentment or anger – are gone. Gone too are any physical disabilities and issues surrounding one's mental health. Any concept of gender is also gone, she says.

Most people see a light, and some even travel into it. Russell says everyone undergoes a life review, playing over what he or she did right and could have been improved upon. There's even the ability to jump back and forth in life and correct any mistakes made, erasing any concept of time whatsoever.

There's also access to a universal knowledge. The answer to every question, from all the mysteries of the universe to quantum physics and even how the universe began, is shared with the experiencer. Unfortunately,

Russell's research suggests most people forget this knowledge when they return to the land of the living.

This covers the similarities between experiences. But what makes each experience different? Based on her research, Russell says the differences occur because each experiencer claims he or she is an active participant in the death event.

"It's not necessarily based on what religion they were raised in," she says, adding she's still trying to make sense of the stories she's been told.

"Some people who are Jewish, for example, will see Jesus. And some times people who are Christians will not have a Christian experience at all. But I want to emphasize that is rare. Very rare. It's mostly that they (the experiencer) follow what they believed."

In a sense, this ties into a theory many spiritualists have thrown around for years; because we view the world through our own subjective experience, we, in essence, create our own reality. This would naturally extend to our death experience as well.

Continuing on, Russell is convinced people have been having near-death experiences for centuries, likely even before the Bible was written. She says people probably didn't understand what was happening to them, nor tried to make sense of the experience, until they essentially "stepped out of the caves" and began creating civilized societies. This is when people turned to, and essentially

JASON HEWLETT & PETER RENN

created, religion as a means of making sense of death, among other things.

"We understand what caused that storm to happen, which destroyed their crops. Or why their beautiful child died of something. They didn't understand death. They didn't understand life. And, of course, there was no science, so they made up stories and that's where the idea of gods came in. They created mythical characters who were responsible for these things," says Russell.

Quite often someone in the community – or tribes as they would have been then – would be designated a shaman or spiritual leader. This person was often the most psychic of the tribe and someone everyone turned to for guidance. The shaman would apply his or her spiritual knowledge to a situation, and even turn to hallucinogens and mild-alerting drugs to aid in the process.

There is a belief among many spiritualists, both in the past and present, that narcotics can shift one's mind into an altered state of consciousness and that this altered state of consciousness allows them to tap into the spiritual side, so to speak, and gain insight from angels and guides. They can even catch glimpses of their past lives, current lives in other parallel dimensions, and see future possible lives they will live. Some believe this other side is where we go during a near-death experience.

So what does all this mean for Russell? Given her

research, does she believe death is the end or the transcendental shift to a new beginning?

"I think there is no such thing as death. We do leave this life, and I guess that can be called anything you want to call it, so death is as good (a name) as any other," she says. "But we don't stop being."

Russell says it's her belief there is only one Spirit or God or Creator or Source, which is her preferred term. We as individuals are all a part of that one source experiencing this existence in order to understand and feel what life is all about from a different perspective instead of "rolling around heaven doing nothing all day."

The deeper Peter and I got into doing the research for this book the more we realized Russell's belief is one that's shared by just about every near-death experiencer we interviewed, as you'll learn as you read through this volume.

When pressed further about the point in this life – which is something each and us have asked ourselves at least once or twice, especially during the COVID-19 pandemic; WHAT IS THE POINT OF ALL THIS!?! – Russell says it's a heady, theological answer. She believes us being on Earth now is partly to learn what life is all about from different perspectives, but at the same time the Source already knows the answer for everything. So, with that in mind, shouldn't we already know everything too?

Yes, she says. However, when we come here, we have

complete amnesia. Many times near-death experiencers will ask a question while at the spirit level. Then when they get the answer, they will say to themselves, "I knew that. How come I forgot?"

"This Source has additional experiences to bounce itself off," says Russell. "So that's what I think we are; we are expressions; we are continuations of being to experience new and different ways of being. Different ways of being. We are a part of all life."

Russell admits it's all a little bit confusing, especially considering the theory we all stem from that one, all-knowing Source. But, if you think about it from a more "down-to-Earth-perspective," as I'll call it, it does make sense.

There's a movement that stems from Eastern religion and philosophy, especially among Zen Buddhists, that talks about oneness; that we are all one, all of humanity is one and simpatico with each other. Russell believes this is the case, but the reality is still much deeper than that.

"There is one soul, one spirit, one entity, and we are it, and we are here to experience being in a different form," she says.

In the end, it's up to us to choose what kind of world – what kind of experience – we want to have and create while we're here, says Russell.

She drew these conclusions after studying a couple of hundred near-death experiences. Taking it back to the beginning, she embarked on this quest to learn what happened when we died, and quickly learned the consistencies of the process, for lack of a better word, once she'd figured that out, Russell wanted to learn the point of it all.

"I started getting this group message," she says.

Based on her research, Russell has ascertained the light people talk about when they return from their near-death experience is the Source, and some people actually go into and become a part of the Source during their experience. She says these people have stated that they see themselves in the act of creation with the Source.

They lose all sense of self, says Russell. They know they've had this life but they are no longer attached to it. It's like an abstract.

"It's like 'I've had that experience, but it's not the authentic me'," she says.

The Source can take different forms too, keeping in line with people having a subjective death experience. Russell says it has taken the forms of friends and family the dying person has known, or even just been a presence that's there with the experiencer but is more of a feeling than anything seen. The Source has even taken the form of people the experiencer was sharing a hospital room with at the time of death.

This is the part that's most fascinating to me; seeing loved ones and acquaintances who have died before you and communicating with them on the other side. There's often a sharing of information that's gone along with these encounters, making amends for grievances unresolved, or hearing answers to questions you needed to know, then a returning to Earth, so to speak. Frequently, near-death experiencers say that almost immediately after death, all grievances they had in life are gone.

On occasion, there's even been warnings about coming tragedies that have, in the end, actually come true, like the death of a loved one or some kind of natural disaster that will impact the experiencer.

Russell believes this is the Source sharing information. But why? She says people often don't want to return to life, and fight the act of being made to do so because it is so beautiful and peaceful and loving on the other side. A love they've never felt before.

"Of course they have. Before this lifetime, they were there. But we forget that," she says.

Now, you might be thinking, and rightly so, this could all be some hallucination or dream caused by the consciousness in a moment of trauma. A coping mechanism, so to speak. And there's a strong argument for that, especially from a neuroscience point of view, which we'll touch on in a future chapter.

If that's the case, though, then how come so many people claim to have this exact same experience, or some variation of it? Skeptics argue the pop culture surrounding near-death experiences is implanting the scenario in people's minds. When suffering a similar traumatic event, the mind "fills in the blanks," so to speak, hence multiple people having the same encounters. The same has been argued for alien abductions and the Old Hag encounters during sleep paralysis.

Given the breadth of her research, Russell is convinced near-death experiences are real and that these people have indeed died and come back to life. Her reasoning is the long list of experiences these people have while being essentially dead.

She explains one incident where an experiencer was in the hospital and pronounced dead. This person saw a child in the next room and was able to diagnose what the child was ill with after they returned to life, and this diagnosis was correct, she says.

"They come back knowing other people who had passed at the same time as them, and no one else new about (them passing) yet. They didn't know that person was dead," says Russell.

People have come back having met siblings or relatives they'd never met in life, or knowing others who had died, such as children who had been stillborn and miscarried, she says.

The human brain does remain active to a degree for up to forty-five minutes after someone has died. However, Russell doesn't believe near-death experiences can be attributed to activity in the brain stem as it breaks down.

The cases that fascinate Russell the most, the ones that convince her beyond a shadow of a doubt near-death experiences are real, are the people who come back hours after being clinically dead. These are the cases where there's no way the brain is still conscious enough to dream the experience up.

"Their bodies are in the morgue and in a state of rigor mortis at the time they come back," says Russell.

Most near-death experiences take place over the span of a couple of minutes but, for the experiencer, feel longer. The reason many occur in a minute or two is because they happen in a hospital where there's a crash cart present, says Russell. The people are brought back to life as soon as possible.

"There's very few who stay dead," she says. "Some do stay dead, and they either don't wake up at all. They don't come back. Or they come back in the morgue."

But Russell has researched cases where people have come back after being dead twelve to fourteen hours, or even longer. She says there's no way the experiences were created by the brain breaking down. In these cases, there is no other possible explanation, and when it comes to the critics and skeptics, they don't examine these incidents further to learn the actual causes. She believes these are the experiences science needs to take a hard look at.

"I'd like to have good quality research done on those elements," says Russell. "That's very important."

Why is science so hesitant to explore the possibility of life after death, and not just near-death experiences but the possibility that people can remain on this plane of existence as a ghost? Russell says science is black and white and scientists must be able to do the same experiment over and over again to quantify the results before they can be taken as fact.

When it comes to near-death experiences in particular, and the paranormal in general, this just isn't possible, she says.

"There's no explanation that makes sense," Russell says. "In the eyes of sciences, if it can't be explored and felt and touched it's disqualified."

As a paranormal investigator, I felt compelled to ask Russell what she thinks ghosts are. If we all go to this Source when we die, then what are these spirits people claim to encounter? She says some souls refuse to leave because they're attached to someone for a particular reason, or they don't know they've died. Then there are other souls who don't feel they're worthy of going into the Source.

One of the cases Russell researched involved a man who had died and was in the tunnel heading up into the light. She says he met souls who were afraid to go into the light and asked them why they weren't going to the light. They responded that they'd been told in life that they weren't worthy based on their religious beliefs.

"They were sinners, and they should not go up into the light," says Russell.

Others have reported being frightened and not understanding what was happening to them, so they don't go to the Source, she says. There's others still who claim they died and found themselves in Hell, so to speak. These people claim to have these horrible experiences happen to them in this place but, if they call out and ask to be removed, they are instantly gone and with the Source.

There was one case where a person found himself in this "Hell" and, although not a religious man, began singing "Jesus loves me, this I know" over and over and instantly found himself moving into the light. When he asked where he'd just been, a soul told him that was a place of his own making, says Russell.

This fits into Russell's explanation of death being a subjective experience. One must also assume a person's religious background also influences the experience. Russell agrees.

"There is no 'Hell.' If you want to create that for your life, go for it," she says. "People talk about our world being Hell. Well, if that's what you want to make it."

If there is a take away from the conversation with Russell, it's that life and death are whatever we want them to be. You want life to be happy, and you work hard to make it so, then that's what it will be. If you believe your life is hard and it is Hell, then this pattern of thinking will influence your death experience.

And, if you believe in nothing, then perhaps that's what you will find on the other side. This is a thought that frightens me more than dying.

CHAPTER FOUR_
DEATH AND CONSCIOUSNESS

WE'VE ALREADY COVERED A LOT OF GROUND IN THIS book, exploring the spiritual and psychological side of death and near-death experiences, as well as taking a deep dive into some of the research done on the subject.

What about the science, the more skeptical among you might be asking? Don't facts and evidence have a place in a book like this? Hard facts, and hard evidence, as the terminology among the skeptical often goes?

Fear not, for as paranormal investigators, that's exactly what Peter and I look for. Or at least we try to find the closest possible thing to hard facts and hard evidence in a field where, as Lynn Russell pointed out, such things are difficult to come by.

We've alluded to mainstream science's thoughts on near-death experience already, but I figured this is the perfect time to talk to a man who's dedicated his life to the study of the mind and its impact on consciousness.

That man is Lawrence Ward, and he's a psychology professor at the University of British Columbia. He began his career in the 1970s studying psychophysics, which is the study of consciousness, as well as psychology in general, and holds a doctor of philosophy.

Ward began studying psychophysics in grad school. He always wanted to be a physicist. However, he didn't believe his math skills were up to that task due to a deprived high school background. So he switched various academic fields, studying psychology, sociology and anthropology and initially attended grad school with the intent of studying social psychology, but quickly became disenchanted when his mathematical approach was discouraged and his deliberately frustrated experimental subjects became mad at him. In the end, Ward found himself in the field of psychophysics where his minor in math was applauded.

"That seemed to be the ideal home for me because I wanted to be doing physics-like stuff but had become interested in psychology as an under grad," says Ward.

Psychophysics is the study of the physics of consciousness. Or, in more scientific terms, it looks at the quantitative relations between psychological events and physical events. More specifically, it explores the relationships between sensations and the stimuli that produce them.

German scientist and philosopher Gustav Theodor Fechner established the science in the middle 1800s, coining the word, developing the fundamental methods, and conducting the psychophysical experiments. The line of investigation he created is still used to this day.

"He wanted to know what the relationship was between the brain and consciousness," says Ward. "He was interested in the philosophy of the mind, but he was a physicist, basically, and a doctor as well, and he wanted to know 'How is brain activity related to consciousness?'"

Fechner began his research from the outside in, so to speak, as there was no way in the middle 1800s to look at the inner workings of the brain. But by looking at the stimulus – how the brain reacts to touch and sound, for example – Theodor made assumptions as to why these reactions were taking place. Ward says this provided Theodor with an early window to how consciousness was influenced by the world around it.

His research took a leap forward after Theodor suffered a mental breakdown, as such episodes were called in those days. Ward says Theodor was in bed recovering and was struck by the idea that, if he made specific kinds of assumptions, he could actually measure consciousness. This led to Theodor inventing psychometrical scaling, which scientists now routinely use to gauge a person's reaction to experiences like the loudness of a sound or the brightness of a light.

This technique has been modified considerably over the years, and Ward's work in psychophysics has contributed to a lot of the changes during his research in the 1970s, `80s and into the `90s.

During the 1990s, Ward's focus shifted to neuroimaging. New techniques were emerging in functional magnetic resonance imaging (FMRI) and the electroencephalogram (EEG), as well as the magnetoencephalography (MEG) was coming on line. All of these different devices allowed scientists and doctors to explore different levels of activity in the brain via brain imaging.

"One of my grad students was getting involved with them and they kind of forced me to get involved," he says jokingly.

Ward set up an EEG lab at the university, and he's been involved in the work ever since while also doing some research using FMRI and MEG.

But there's more. Ward has another interest which stems from his involvement with "a group of people who wanted to look at theories of critical phenomena." He says an event like an earthquake or avalanche is caused by one slight "slippage" in the land, or along a mountain, but the effect of that slight change can have widespread repercussions.

"Well, the same thing is true of consciousness," he says. "Consciousness is a critical phenomenon and slight changes in the way the brain is acting can affect consciousness. And since I was interested in consciousness I got involved in this group."

One of the things the group studied was the affect of noise on all sorts of different phenomena, and that led Ward back to his interest in physics. Since then he's worked alongside scientists and mathematicians and published a lot of work on how the brain oscillates, and how these oscillations are related to consciousness and how the brain creates consciousness.

This last paragraph should give you an idea of where Ward's bias is when it comes to exploring and explaining near-death experiences.

"I don't feel that it's very useful to postulate that there is something other than the universe," he says. "To me the universe means the universe. It means everything."

While Ward's story so far, and the research he's done, might exclude things like near-death experiences from being a legitimate phenomenon, he does appreciate the work being done on the multiverse theory.

This theory hypothesizes there are a group of multiple universes that, together, comprises everything that exists. The entirety of space, time, matter, energy, information, and the physical laws and constants that describe them are within these multiple, possible universes. This suggests our universe, with its hundreds of billions of galaxies and countless stars and planets spanning ten-billion light years, may not be the only one.

All of this hasn't been tested yet, but science is taking a good hard look at the possibility ours is just one of countless realities. Which means there's more than one you and me out there, and we're potentially living untold parallel lives.

Suffice to say, many paranormal researchers are all over the multiverse theory as it potentially explains déjà vu, reincarnation and the existence of ghosts, Bigfoot, and other cryptids. Everything paranormal could be a result of multiverse theory.

"I think it's an amazing concept," says Ward, adding just because we haven't yet made contact with any of these parallel universes doesn't mean they don't exist.

There are a variety of interpretations of multiverse theory, one of the most common being the world splits every time one of us makes a conscious decision to do, or not do, something. Ward believes this idea is not the same thing as the potential existence of a multiverse.

"The multiverse is more the idea that there are maybe about ten to the sixtieth different possible universes as allowed by string theory and other esoteric theories," he says. "They have different energy levels, and they spawn each other, and they might not all be coexistent at the same time. There can be only a relative few of them."

Continuing on, Ward believes there's only a few different possible universes in existence at the same time, and most of them wouldn't have anything close to our type of universe, with an Earth like ours etcetera.

Then there's Omega Point Theory, which Ward says is quite controversial. This theory was inspired by the language of Jesuit paleontologist Pierre Teilhard de Chardin and later put forward by physicist and mathematician Frank Tipler in a series of articles published during the 1980s. Tipler begins with the Big Bang, then theorizes the universe will eventually, after hundreds of billions of years, converge to an infinite all-knowing point at the end of universe and the end of time. When this happens, God-like observers will have the ability to perform tasks in infinite time.

"They will be able to reanimate every living thing that had ever existed before, at least in emulation," says Ward.

This theory is a way of reconciling religion and physics at the same time, Ward says, while taking into account that no universe can exist without humanity. The ultimate aim is to show that we're immortal, which ties into the idea of life after death and near-death experiences.

Even when taking omega and multiverse theories into account, Ward remains convinced death is the end. He says his beliefs align with a book called *The Little Book of Atheist Spirituality*, which was written by French philosopher Andre Comte-Sponville. This book questions God's existence while acknowledging the good that has come from religion. It asks for tolerance of religious believers and nonbelievers alike and appeals for a new form a spirituality based on the human need to connect with each other and the universe.

"He's arguing you can be an atheist and not believe in any gods or any life after death or anything like that and still have a high degree of spirituality," says Ward. "He puts a lot of emphasis on silence and stillness and having these transcendental experiences as a spiritual experience but not necessarily having anything to do with the continuation of your life (after death)."

The point is to make your life awe inspiring and meaningful now while you're alive, says Ward, who has had a number of transcendental experiences himself, including some that could be classified as out-of-body experiences.

For the uninitiated, an out-of-body experience is one in which a person has a feeling of being separated from his or her body and is able to look at himself or herself and other people from outside the body.

For Ward, it's all a matter of consciousness, or different levels of consciousness. Does a person appear to have consciousness when they are dead? he asks. No. The same is true of someone who has suffered severe trauma to the brain. But there are some cases where questions can be asked of a patient who is comatose, and the brain responds.

"You can ask them to change their brain activity in a specific way and the brain will do it," he says, adding this occurs in only a few cases. "They appear to have some level of consciousness because they are able to respond to our requests."

Once a person stops behaving, however, and when they stop being able to manipulate their own brain activity on request, there is no way to know what is going on inside their heads, says Ward. He's done research on dying people and has found evidence that, in some cases where these people are unresponsive, there are still indications they are listening to things when they are dying. This has even gone on after these people have died.

There are also cases called active dying, where a person is dying a natural death and doctors are unable to take good measurements of everything that is going on in the person's body during the process. Ward says people can enter into "strange states" during death where their metabolic rate slows down to the point they appear dead but are still barely alive.

He's not sure how long these states can last without causing damage to the heart, but there have been cases where people have drowned in ice-cold water and been resuscitated after ten or even twenty minutes.

"They should've been dead, and they would've been dead had they just been warm and their brain would've started dying," says Ward.

In these incidences, it was the cold that prolonged the person's life when he or she is at the brink of death, he says. This is where science fiction authors came up with the concept of cryogenic sleep.

The bottom line with every single case like this is when the brain doesn't get enough oxygen, there is damage done, starting in the thalamus and sub cortex regions before moving to the cortex. Ward says as certain areas of the brain start to die, there's this "critical mass" that takes place; then the brain stops functioning.

When people are truly brain dead, there is no metabolic activity whatsoever in the brain. He says these people never wake up again.

"There's never been a case of that," says Ward.

There are tests doctors do to test for full brain death in the sub cortex, like poking fingers with needles and manipulating the eyes – procedures even an unconscious patient would instinctively react to. When these fail to generate a response, medical personnel are fairly certain there's no metabolic activity going on even at the sub cortex level of the brain. Ward says that gives doctors permission to take a patient off life support.

As far as Ward is aware, there's never been a recorded case of a patient being brain dead and then coming back to life.

"There have been cases of people being kept alive in a coma, and that's very different," he says. "In those cases the person's brain is still alive... And there are cases, and they're not too common, of people coming out of a coma directly."

Usually people kept alive in a coma come out of that state into death, or transition into an unresponsive state of wakefulness, which used to be known as a vegetative state. If these people are lucky, they eventually progress to a state of minimal responsiveness, says Ward. From there, people either die, remain in this condition of minimal responsiveness, or recover with some deficiencies.

The problem with most of these outcomes is the diagnosis is done by neurologists using bed-side tests that are not very accurate. In fact, about forty-five percent of people diagnosed as vegetative or unresponsive wakefulness were actually conscious. Ward says the neurologists do their best, and perform multiple tests multiple times, but a person with brain damage has a fluctuating arousal state, meaning some times they are more responsive to stimulus than at other times.

"This is the case with a minimally responsive state. People drift in and out of consciousness in a minimally conscious state," he says.

If this person is only conscious for fifteen minutes a day every other day or every fourth day, there's a slim chance a neurologist is going to hit that moment, says Ward. These people can then be labelled unresponsive when they are indeed conscious to a degree.

"We know people aren't always totally unconscious,"

Ward says. "That's one of the things with the near-death experiences that's problematic."

Anyone who claims to have come back from being clinically dead wasn't clinically dead, he says. If you're really dead, your body starts to rot. And as far as Ward is concerned, that's the one true sign of death.

Ward argues people who say they've had these near-death experiences are using an "index of death" that's not accounting for the fact they haven't actually died and their body begun to rot. There's some level of consciousness there, and that's what creates the near-death experience.

He even estimates that ninety-eight percent of the time or ninety-nine point nine percent of the time it might appear that someone's heart has stopped beating, but in reality, it's the pulse that can't be found.

"You don't know what the heart's doing really. You're just measuring a peripheral event that you think is correlating with the heart rate," says Ward. "So you can't find the heart rate for ten minutes. Does that mean the person's dead? No."

For a person to be truly dead, Ward reiterates, there needs to be no pulse, no breath, and the brain and body have begun to rot. He says it takes more than a few minutes for all three to take place and during those few minutes the brain, is definitely conscious and active.

Yes, the brain does start to suffer when the heart stops. But there's no guarantee it will suffer permanent damage if the person is resuscitated after a few minutes, says Ward. And, once again, the brain is still functioning during that time.

"There's all sorts of different circumstances that affect how quickly the brain starts to die," he says.

Many of the times a person has been revived after a fatal occurrence outside of a hospital there has been some brain damage as a result, and often the damage is so minor only a skilled neuropsychologist will notice, he says. Even then this person would have to be highly intelligent and highly active.

If a cardiologist is resuscitating a patient in a hospital, they are about ninety-five percent successful in reviving the person with no brain damage at all.

"There's a better chance of somebody pulling through in the hospital," says Ward.

All these different variables contribute to so many people believing they've had a near-death experience when, in fact, it's the creation of a person's consciousness during these various "indexes of dying," he says. For Ward, death is indeed the end, and our consciousness doesn't go on past that. When the body dies, the specific conditions needed for consciousness are simply no longer there.

"I'm using consciousness as a proxy for what people I guess would call the soul or essence of the person," he says. "It's our awareness of the world but, even more than that, our awareness of ourselves in the world. That is what is at issue here."

What people need to do while alive is be in tune with, and awed by, the simple fact we're able to ask such profound questions as what happens when we die. He says we have the opportunity to observe ourselves, the world, and the universe and that is something we shouldn't squander by focusing on the trivialities of life.

"We should be aware of that all the time but, of course, we don't all the time. We're just doing our own thing most of the time," says Ward.

Conversing with Ward is a stimulating experience and, although he doesn't believe near-death experiences or life after death is possible, it doesn't take long to appreciate his message that the life we have is one that shouldn't be squandered.

What I'm still curious about, though, are his thoughts on the commonalities reported by those who claim to have had a near-death experience. The tunnel of light, the presence of other beings, communicating telepathically and so on. If these experiences aren't real, why are so many people explaining the same phenomenon?

The answers, he says, can be found in what happens to the brain as it begins to die. When dying a natural death, you will have a decrease in the supply of blood to the brain. He speculates this causes a sequence of events in the brain as it shuts down, much like the sun during a sunset.

"During a sunset, as it gets darker and darker and darker, there is sort of a progression in things that you lose visually," he says, adding the brain operates on a series of networks that interact with each other, sending information back and forth in order to sustain consciousness.

He says speculates because a study has yet to be done on what exactly happens to the brain as it shuts down during death. Why? Because this would be very difficult to do.

As the brain begins to shut down, some of those networks are probably more vulnerable to loss of information flow than others. Ward believes it's this shutdown of networks within the brain that causes the phenomenon people are describing, and why it's reported by so many experiencers.

"There is some sort of sequence (in the dying brain) that is more or less the same for all people when they're dying this kind of death, and when they come back, they have of course experienced part of a sequence but not all of it, otherwise they wouldn't be coming back," says Ward.

It's been noted in patients suffering from dementia that the parts of the brain that govern reasoning and decision making are the first to go, he says. What remains are images and memories that play out like a dream without anything to apply reason to what's being seen by the experiencers. Essentially the brain is running in "default mode," and this creates the visuals near-death experiencers have.

This "default mode" has been found to function in palliative care or unresponsive patients hours after they've died, says Ward.

"I would argue this type of thing is what's responsible for these images in people with near-death experiences," he says.

Given the prevalence of near-death experiences reported in the media, and discussions on television and in documentaries, Ward believes one would have to go into the deep Amazon in order to find someone who doesn't know something about them. This knowledge is likely subconsciously applied to the experience one has, almost like a memory.

This does make sense to me, as people are very good at putting ideas together to create a narrative that works for them and brings them comfort. With that in mind, someone injured in a car accident who feels they are on the brink of death could create this near-death event because that's what is "supposed to happen."

Ward agrees, adding suggestion is a very powerful motivator for people.

"When you are then asked to remember (what happened) suggestion is also a powerful motivator then," he says.

To do research in this field of study, really good research, one has to be very aware of all the possible biases that can come up, Ward says, providing some good advice before we log off.

Our conversation is one that's provided a nice counterpoint to the ones we've had so far, which appeals to the journalist in me. Too often one side of the story is reported, especially when it comes to subjects like this one, where each side has a firm stance for or against what they believe in.

What's also interesting is the spiritual nature Ward brings to the subject, even as a non-believer in near-death experiences. This is rare among scientists and academics I've met.

Before we turn to another academic for their thoughts on the subject, I think it would be good to hear a powerful story of one man's encounter with the other side.

CHAPTER FIVE_
A SHARED-DEATH EXPERIENCE

So far we've talked about near-death experiences that have happened to an individual; that is, someone dies, or allegedly dies, and comes back to talk about it. But there's another kind of death experience called a shared-death experience, where a loved one or caregiver feels like he or she has participated in a dying person's transition to the other side.

Although not as widely reported as near-death experiences, this is a very real phenomenon that has been underreported in hospice and palliative care medicine, likely because it sounds even more farfetched than the near-death experiences we've talked about so far.

Nonetheless, such experiences have been documented, with experiencers claiming four distinct, though nonexclusive types of shared-death experience: remotely sensing a death, witnessing unusual phenomena, feelings of accompanying the dying, and feelings of assisting the dying to the other side.

The effects these experiences have on the person sharing the death experience are profound, including changes in spiritual belief, the reconciliation of grief, and the perception of continuing a bond with the deceased.

I was lucky enough to meet a man who believes he's had a shared-death experience. Scott Taylor says the event profoundly changed his life, and prompted a lifelong quest to understand what happened to him and why.

Taylor says he's now able to practice a form of meditation that allows him to go back to "that exquisite place again," meaning he can travel to the other side any time he wants. While this might sound farfetched, other near-death experiencers claim to do the same thing, and we'll hear from them later in this book.

His ability to do this has resulted in a thirty-six-year career as a trainer for the Monroe Institute, a nonprofit organization which, since 1974, has offered guided programs that use a sound technology to empower people on their journey of self-discovery. For two years Taylor acted as the institute's president and executive director.

Taylor also holds a doctorate in educational leadership at the University of Saint Thomas in Minnesota, had an extensive career in retail and as an entrepreneur, and has been a mentor for other entrepreneurs.

His dissertation was about near-death experiences, as

Taylor had a desire to explore spirituality in his paper. His dean encouraged him to explore the subject, as his neighbor had such an experience. At first, Taylor wasn't sure he wanted to write about such a thing. However, it seems the universe had the answer for him.

On the drive to a friend's that day, he heard an interview on the radio about near-death experiences. When he arrived at his friend's house, she opened the door, and before he could say anything, she told him she was listening to an interesting show on near-death experiences – the same one he was listening to in the car. Later during the same visit, he noticed a book on his friend's night stand that was about, you guessed it, near-death experiences.

"So I went 'Alright, I'm going to look into this and see how it goes.'" he says.

As with writing and researching any topic for a dissertation, there's a large amount of reading involved. Taylor says he read pretty much every book he could find on near-death experiences, but it was a volume he picked off the shelf in a bookstore in Washington State that was a game changer for him.

The book was thin with a black binding and caught his eye amongst the other books on the shelf. So he grabbed the book, which was written by P. M. H. Atwater, opened it up, and began thumbing through pages. He paused somewhere in the thirteenth chapter and came across one little paragraph that read "Sometimes when people are bedside with those making their transition, the person bedside leaves their physical body and goes to the light with that person and they share that experience together. And that's called a shared near-death experience or an empathetic-death experience."

Stunned, Taylor thought to himself, "That's what happened to me!"

Up until that time, Taylor didn't know that what happened to him back in 1981 was a near-death experience. He says it was so outside of anything that had been written about near-death experiences to assume he'd had one.

He'd initially dismissed the experience because everything written up to and including 1981 involved people who had suffered severe physical trauma to their own body and the body died. Taylor's didn't. He was in a hospital room when someone he loved left his body for the last time.

"None of it fit with what a near-death experience was until I read that book," says Taylor. "And I went 'Holy smokes. I have a home.'"

Suddenly there was a body of literature supporting what had happened to Taylor all those years ago. He felt it was serendipity that he was writing about the subject for his dissertation and it was only while researching the topic that he found out it had indeed happened to him.

"It was backwards in how you'd usually think about.

Usually you'd think, 'I had one, I read about it, and I want to investigate it further'. It wasn't that way at all," says Taylor.

Taylor is among a rare group of people who believe they had a shared-death experience, but he also says he's among the few who have had a light experience as well. This light can be white, black or clear, with a white light being the most commonly reported. His involved a clear light, which is the rarest kind of light reported.

So what happened to Taylor? Back in 1981 he was in love with Mary Fran and her son, Nolan, who had just turned seven. Mother and son were driving home after a summer's day spent sailing, and Mary Fran attempted to make a left-hand turn onto a two-lane country road.

The setting sun blinded her, and she pulled out in front of an oncoming car, which struck the driver's door, killing her instantly. Nolan sustained severe head trauma and was taken to St. Mary's Hospital in Rochester, Minnesota.

Mortally wounded, he fought to live for six days, but it was a battle he could not win.

Nolan was the first grandchild in a family of nine children. During the days he battled to stay alive, friends and relatives had time to visit him in hospital and lend support, comfort and prayers.

"There were brothers and sisters, uncles and aunts, grandparents and cousins, spouses and significant others, girlfriends and friends, her family and my family. We kept an around-the-clock-vigil at his bedside," he says.

He and Mary Fran's sister, Janney, had the three to five a.m. shift on the sixth morning after the accident. Taylor says they read Nolan's unconscious body stories, told him about all the friends and relatives who had come to support him, and they comforted him as best they could.

Janney is a registered nurse with years of experience in trauma care, he says. She looked at Nolan's chart and vital signs, which were displayed on the many electronic monitors. It was clear to her where Nolan's vital signs were heading.

"With tears brimming in her eyes, Janney held out her hand to me and gently pulled me into the chair by Nolan's head," Taylor says, tears in his eyes as he tells the story. "It's time," she said.

"Janney leaned over and whispered in his ear, 'Nolan, you've been a very good and very brave boy. It's okay to go and join your mother. It's okay for you to leave. You have fought so hard and been such a good boy. It's okay to leave. We love you.'"

With this, Taylor said his goodbyes, and both left Nolan's room and joined the sleeping relatives camped out on the chairs and sofas in the waiting room. Taylor says forty-five minutes passed and Nolan's nurse woke everyone from his or her fitful sleep and quietly told them it was time to say goodbye.

Taylor is almost overwhelmed with emotion as he continues his story, saying so many family members were gathered that, by the time he entered the room, there were three rows of people around the bed. He found a spot to sit on the window sill next to Mary Fran's youngest sibling, Willy.

As Nolan's heartbeat patterns flattened and the monitor beside his bed sounded the constant, unwavering tone of organ failure, every member of the boy's extended family wept.

"Except for me," says Taylor.

As Nolan left his physical body, Taylor watched as Mary Fran crossed the divide between the physical and nonphysical world and scooped up his body, he says.

"Their reunion embrace was exquisite," he says, weeping openly. "Then, to my surprise, Mary Fran and Nolan turned and included me in their embrace. Together the three of us went to the light."

There are no words that can describe the combination of joy, ecstasy, love and requited longing that Taylor felt burning inside him, he says. The sensation carried him to a dimension he never knew existed.

"In that moment, there was no pain of loss, only unity, rapture and reunion," he says.

"I was overcome with an indescribable joy and love that transported me into a realm where ecstasy is a pale description of what I felt. Where I went, I had no idea at the time. I was fully conscious, fully present in the hospital room with the grieving family. Yet, simultaneously, I was lifted to a place beyond description."

He says he experienced bilocation, two fully conscious vantage points. One was on the window sill next to Willy; the second somewhere in another dimension, embraced by Mary Francis and Nolan as she guided her son farther into the light.

While in the light, Taylor was also fully present in a roomful of quietly grieving family members. He knows this because he realized how inappropriate he felt he was being. Taylor was filled with joy, he says.

"So much so I thought my face would break from the inner force of ecstasy trying to get out," says Taylor.

So he did the only thing he could think of: he covered his face with his hands in order for that radiance of joy not to be noticed. Taylor says the expression was not only inappropriate, it would have been entirely misunderstood given the family lost Mary Francis with a week and Nolan just moments before.

"I stayed with the two of them as long as I could. Then it was time to go, and I gently rejoined my body in the hospital ward some minutes later," says Taylor.

Taylor felt it would be inappropriate to share his experience with anyone because it didn't fit the profound grief everyone was feeling at that moment. He also couldn't put the experience into words either. At the time, he had no frame of reference with which to describe the event, so he kept quiet for twenty years.

"I thought I knew how the world worked," he says. "My experience with Nolan's transition wasn't described in any religious or secular literature of which I was aware. It wasn't part of my family's belief structure or the lexicon of the Presbyterian Church in which I was raised. As a result, I was totally unprepared for the consequences of my experience and my radically altered worldview."

When it's come to Taylor's work, he's always found himself in a leadership role, so he believes his death experience was reflective of that. He says leadership comes from the inside out, and whatever you believe about the world and how it works – whether it's to be feared or not – has a profound effect on who you are as a person and how you present yourself to those around you.

As a result of his experience, Taylor now sees himself and the world through a lens of unity and oneness. He says all a person has to do is touch that light on the other side for a second to experience that sensation. In the end, this became the subject of his dissertation, which he completed eight years ago.

What Peter and I discovered while researching this book is many experiencers come back reporting that same sensation of love, peace, calmness and unity, and many are profoundly changed by it. There's a new appreciation of life and who they are, and less of a need to fit in with society, as you'll read about later in this volume.

Whether this change is a result of what they experience on the other side, or simply a newfound appreciation for being alive, remains to be seen.

Why does Taylor believe all this happened to him? If shared-death experiences are so rare, why was he fortunate enough to have one? Taylor's research into shared-death experiences suggests there's two components needed: a strong bond between the person making the transition and the person bedside.

"This was the case with Nolan. He'd never known his biological father, so I'd kinda stepped into that role and we were starting to form that bond," he says. "And of course there was Mary Fran."

The second component is the person making the transition wants the third party to join them, Taylor says.

"They invited me. That seems to be the key, that the person making the transition reached back and invited me into that experience," he says.

Why would a person want that? Are they not ready to transition to the other side, or are they seeking comfort from someone as they make the journey?

Taylor takes a moment to respond, weighing his answer. Then he suggests having someone join them is about sharing this "exquisite experience" and honoring the relationship between the dying person and the one left behind.

"It's kinda like 'You're gonna want to know what's happened to us, and this is it,'" he says.

Taylor admits he's still emotional about the tragic death of Mary Francis and Nolan, even after all these years, and that he understands people might take what he's saying as a way of grieving their loss and continuing on with life. But he says there's also this joy and euphoria that came with the shared-death experience, and he believes it happened.

"What was hard for me for a long time was how could I at the moment of my greatest grief be in my greatest joy? These two emotions for me now are inextricably linked," he says.

This greatest joy is being able to touch what Taylor describes as the "exquisite love of the universe." But what does he think it is, this other place filled with peace, love and oneness? What Taylor saw is in line with other experiences described in this book, and by near-death experiencers. Is it the brain releasing chemicals while it dies in order to make the transition into death easier? Or did he, Mary Francis and Nolan travel to the other side?

"What we're doing is stepping into the nonphysical universe," he says. "It has different rules than the physical universe and the vibration of the universe is love. Full stop. End of sentence. There is nothing else."

Vibration is a word you'll read many times in pages to come, suggesting this "other side" exists very close to ours and is accessible by almost "tuning into a different frequency," so to speak.

Any suggestion these experiences are a result of dopamine or some vague memory of the birth canal is ridiculous to Taylor, who believes science has pretty much disproven these theories. He says Bruce Greyson's work on the subject of near-death experiences closed the book on such ideas.

Greyson is the world's leading expert on near-death experiences. A physician with no religious belief system, he approaches these experiences from a scientific perspective and, after four decades of research, came to the conclusion death could be the threshold from one form of consciousness to another, not an ending but a transition. Through his research, he discovered several common and universal themes in near-death experiences that go beyond neurophysiological or cultural interpretations.

His latest book, *After*, lays out the scientific case for near-death experiences, and lays to rest any doubts as to what happens, says Taylor.

Peter and I reached out to Greyson to be interviewed for this book, but he did not answer our requests.

According to Greyson, by way of Taylor and other near-death experiencers, we have a nonphysical body, we inhabit a nonphysical body for a while, and when the physical body dies, we go back into the non-physical world.

"That's home. That's where we come from. That's where we return to," says Taylor. "This world here, this physical world we inhabit, is a minute portion of the nonphysical universe."

So why are we here? If we are created in this space of oneness and love what is the point of taking physical form and existing somewhere that, at times, seems the exact opposite of this wonderful place we're eventually going to return to?

Taylor answers in one word: contrast.

"The way I see it, we come from a universe that is unity, where everything is connected to everything else and, as such, all you know is the love of the universe. And you have to step away from that and into a world of contrast so you can appreciate and learn what it's like to have duality," he says.

It's here in this physical world where we learn about good and evil and all of the contrast that exist, says Taylor. This includes individuality, as there's no Jason and Scott on the other side. We exist there, but without the individual characteristics that make us unique from one another.

"We are different people (there), but we are also the same person. We are all part of the whole," says Taylor.

This seems very much in line with the Buddhist belief

in Taoism, which holds that humans and animals should live in balance with the Tao, or universe, and where the spirit of the body joins the universe after death.

Taylor goes on to explain the rules of the universe, saying in the physical world – the world of duality – things are governed by the words either and or. For example, you go to sit on a chair. There is you and the chair. Both are different. But, in the nonphysical world, there is you and the chair, but you are also one and the same.

"Yes that is a chair that is separate, I am me, and we are also made up of the same stuff, the vibration and love of the universe," he says.

I am compelled to ask Taylor if we were conversing in the nonphysical world, would we see each other as we currently are, or would we be in a bright light with an awareness of each other. He says we'd see each other as separate but also be one. There would be total communication between the two of us, but it would be wordless.

All communication is telepathic, as we are all one and can share common thoughts, says Taylor.

Which brings Taylor and me to the elephant in the room, at least for religious people. Given his experience, and the experiences of thousands – if not tens of thousands – of near-death experiencers, is there any validity to religion, or is it a construct we made up to help make sense of things we couldn't at the time explain? Taylor's answer isn't surprising.

Religion is something we came up with to explain our experiences, he says.

Taylor continues, echoing concepts Lynn Russell mentioned in the previous chapter, and describes a vibrational level where bewildered souls who are caught unaware at the time of death hang out until they "get their bearings" and can move on.

There are, in fact, beings called Soul Rescuers who help these bewildered souls find their way into the light, he says.

"Coming from the physical into the nonphysical takes some getting used to," he says.

He goes on to describe "a whole center" where souls get to recover from the traumas they suffered in the physical world, be they mental illness, severe disease, or injuries as a result of violence or accident. After a while, people identify themselves with these traumas, and that defines the person's life. This Healing and Regeneration Center helps people put these traumas behind them and transition into the light.

As a paranormal investigator I wondered if the activity Peter and I encounter during our investigations is caused by those bewildered souls who aren't ready to move into the light, or who haven't gone through the Healing and Regeneration Center. Taylors believes they are, saying these are souls who want to remain on the Earthly realm.

"Maybe you want to be there for your children. Maybe

the trauma that you had locks you into a certain place or a house. Or you're just so Earthbound in your thinking that you chose to remain at the lower vibrational level," he says.

Once a soul is shown the light by a Soul Rescuer, paranormal investigator or psychic, they immediately want to transition over, says Taylor. They no longer see a need to remain behind.

All of this does sound hard to swallow, the reasoning of which is a direct result of the way our modern society views death. We're scared of it, especially those who don't believe in anything, be it religion, ghosts or what have you. If you don't believe there's anything after death, then any notion of life after it is a moot point.

Taylor argues these are the souls who don't – or can't – move on. He finds this sad as, from his experience, death isn't the end at all but a transition.

My work has me convinced there is more to life than this physical world. And while I have a hard time grasping the concept of a Healing and Regeneration Center, Taylor talks about his experience with such honest conviction I have a hard time discounting his experience, especially after almost twenty years as a paranormal investigator and a decade as a mainstream journalist with an ear for bullshit.

Taking a cue from Lawrence Ward, I question Taylor about the multiverse concept, asking him how it fits into his point of view, if at all. Taylor says it does.

"It's my belief that we exist on all planes of existence at once," he says, describing these planes of existence as vibratory levels. "Our souls exist in all of them all of the time."

So we're currently talking on the physical plane of existence but, at the same time, interacting with our deceased relatives in the nonphysical. Meanwhile, our soul is also having a life elsewhere on a different plane of existence that's available to us, he says.

People can train themselves in the physical world to change their vibratory level so they can commune with deceased relatives in the nonphysical realm. Taylor says this is done through meditation.

Having practiced meditation for years, and spoken with many who have dedicated a lifetime to the study, what Taylor describes certainly isn't out of the realm of the possible. I personally haven't communed with a dead relative while meditating, but I have asked important life questions when entering a meditative state and come back with the answers I've needed. These answers led me to make the right choice at the right time, with positive results.

I've spoken with many others who have gained similar insights, and as you'll read later in this book, there are people who have discovered past lives and spoken with the dead during meditation as well.

Taylor says a near-death experiencer will often come back with the ability to travel to these different vibratory levels. This includes coming back with the ability to "rewind," as he calls it.

During a near-death experience, the experiencer is partnered with a guide whose job it is "to love you through that experience of the life review." This review takes the experiencer through their life, reviewing the good and bad times you've had and the good and bad things you've done and how those affected others.

This review is done without judgment and provides the experiencer the opportunity to view how an encounter would play out if the experiencer had responded differently, Taylor says.

"The guide can take and play that scene the second way where you were the nice guy and a compassionate person instead of being a jerk who snipped at the trainee at the grocery store," says Taylor.

"The cool part is that when we have these little rewinds, that experience where I'm a nice guy instead of being a jerk, that's also now part of the human experience. Just as much as the first experience where I was a jerk to the trainee at the grocery store."

The chance to replay and change scenarios in a life review is fascinating, and does play into the multiverse theory where each decision we make creates a different possible universe. To me it sounds like déjà vu, when one feels like they've been somewhere and done something before.

Taylor thinks of it like a time loop given that in the nonphysical universe, all time occurs at the same time.

"Anything is available to us. Any thing and any where," he says. "I think, for a second there, we tap into that timeless nature and go 'Oh, I've lived this before.' Yeah, you have."

Taylor believes it's difficult to describe a near-death experience, but I think he's done a pretty good job. A lot of what he's talked about at first seems out there, for lack of a better word, but so much of it also aligns with what many other experiencers have described. Much like the world of ghost hunting, things seem crazy at first until you realize how many people have experienced the same thing. And then you have an experience yourself.

As I mentioned at the beginning of the book, I haven't had a near-death experience per se, but Peter has, and I think now is a good time to tell his story.

CHAPTER SIX_
PETER'S STORY

GIVEN PETER RENN HAS SPENT ALMOST THIRTY YEARS of his life investigating paranormal activity around the world, it should come as no surprise he'd be interested in the concept of the afterlife.

But Peter, who has lived through the deaths of his parents and sister, believes he touched the other side shortly before receiving the liver transplant that saved his life in early 2018.

We chronicled much of his story in the 2020 bestseller *I Want to Believe: One Man's Journey into the Paranormal.* Peter hails from England, and struggled with alcohol for years, as many of the men in his family have. This resulted in increased illnesses as liver disease caused his organ to fail, even when he gave up the bottle not long after relocating to Canada. He was diagnosed with liver disease in 2008.

During his time as a paranormal investigator, and in his life in general, Peter had plenty of experiences where he was certain he encountered proof of life after death. Two, which we'll detail here, occurred when his mother and grandmother passed away.

Peter's mom died after a battle with cancer. He was living at home on the night she passed away, and had returned late from a day at work. His bedroom was next door to the one where his parents slept. He says his mom wasn't on his mind this particular night, as he was wiped out from work.

He told me he had a vivid dream about his mom coming into his room to see him and say goodbye. She gave him a hug, and he remembers getting quite emotional, even asking where she was going. Then he woke up.

The first thing Peter saw when he opened his eyes was his mom standing at the end of his bed, smiling. He closed his eyes and opened them again, and she was gone. Then his dad knocked on the bedroom door and told him his mother had died during the night.

Peter's paternal grandmother died when he was nine or ten, but it took his parents the better part of a day to let their children know. His mother didn't even say a word to her two children when she picked them up from school and drove them home that same day.

Peter and his sister sat down in front of the TV on the floor, propped up on pillows and watching a program. Off to one side of the television was a doorway to the family's game room. Out of the corner of his eye, Peter saw a figure standing by the sliding doors to the game room. He turned and looked, and there was his grandmother.

Peter remembers turning away from his grandmother and looking to his mom, who stood facing the game room, like she could see the grandmother as well. His mother's jaw had dropped, and her face was white, he says.

"What's Nan doing here?" Peter asked his mother.

"I don't know. I don't know what she's doing here," his mother replied, still pale.

He turned away from his mom and looked back at the game room. His nana was gone.

His mom said she had something to tell the children once Dad got home. Peter's dad arrived a short time later and broke down in tears. It was his mother, Peter's grandmother, who had died.

As a paranormal investigator, he's heard countless stories about near-death experiences. His skeptical mind took this as one story being bounced from person to person after each suffered a traumatic experience.

That all changed during the decade he waited for a liver transplant. As Peter describes it, he "hit ground zero" nine times during the ten years, essentially having a near-death experience almost once a year.

"Over the course of that decade, before my transplant, I was in and out of hospital quite a considerable amount of time with blood poisoning, various problems with my liver. It was malfunctioning," he says.

The final one occurred after Peter fell deathly ill in October 2017. I remember this well, as he and I had just met, and he invited me to join him for an investigation at an allegedly haunted hotel in the Interior of British Columbia. I was to catch a ride to the location with Peter, but he grew too sick to travel.

We actually didn't meet face-to-face until February 2019, but I followed Peter's transplant experience via social media as his wife, Janina, was generous enough to keep all of us posted on his progress. No one learned the extent of what Peter went through, or how close he came to death, until he was well on the way to recovery.

Things took a turn for the worse following a trip to Vancouver, British Columbia. Peter worked for a large construction firm at the time and oversaw major projects for the company. He'd travelled to the coast to pick up a wall for a new hotel in the province's Interior when he began to get a coppery taste in his mouth.

"Uh-oh. It feels like I'm bleeding inside again," he remembers saying to himself. "It was kind of a common trend over this last decade (before the transplant)."

Peter phoned work, told them what was going on, and said he was going straight home. He says these episodes would often pass on their own without a trip to the hospital, which he hoped to avoid.

As soon as he got home, Peter went to bed and fell asleep within minutes. However, when he woke up, his condition had worsened. In fact, he quickly slipped into what he describes as a "state of euphoria" complete with vivid hallucinations. His wife immediately phoned an ambulance and Peter was taken to the hospital.

It turns out Peter had an infection in his liver. He was given medication to treat it and sent home, he says.

A week went by, one Peter spent most of asleep. He says he was supposed to return to work on the Monday, but suffered blood poisoning, which essentially put him out of his mind.

"I was in a bad state. I didn't even know what day it was," says Peter, adding he was stumbling about the home in an almost trance-like state.

He was so out of his mind he was terrifying their two young children, Mason and Emma, he says.

"Janina was saying to me, 'Get into the room, get into the bedroom,' because the kids were scared," says Peter, mimicking the way he stumbled about his home at the time.

"And then I pushed her out of the way."

Fortunately, his father-in-law was there and able to get Peter under control until paramedics arrived to take him to hospital.

This is where Peter's memory becomes a big foggy. He remembers the paramedics picking him up, then being put

JASON HEWLETT & PETER RENN

into a hospital bed, and Janina holding his hand, but that's it.

"I was just totally out. I can't give a duration or anything like that," Peter says.

Eventually the darkness of his comatose state turned white, he says. As Peter describes it, he was walking in another domain towards a half circle of souls with a doorway standing in front of the half circle. Standing within the doorway was another soul.

"The reason why I say souls is because I knew who these people were, but I didn't see facial features or anything like that," says Peter. "But I knew who they were. The person standing in front of me, I knew who he was, but it wasn't me saying, 'Oh hello, John' or anything like that."

Peter felt drawn to the doorway behind the soul guarding it, for lack of a better work. However, when he arrived the soul would not let him pass. The soul told Peter telepathically that he could not come through the door.

"You're not ready to come through," the soul said.

"I need to go through now. I want to go," Peter demanded. "I want to see my mom. I want to see my dad. I want to see my sister."

The soul was insistent, telling Peter he wasn't done with life on Earth yet. Peter isn't sure how long this back-and-forth went on for, but in his mind it felt like the argument continued for a good two minutes. He says in reality it could have gone on for seconds or hours of real time.

However long it went on for, the soul became increasingly angry with Peter for wanting to abandon the life he had. And that's when Peter clued in he was speaking with his long-dead grandfather.

"Even though I'd never met my grandfather, that was my grandfather there," he says, adding the soul displayed all the characteristics he'd been told about his grandfather.

"I didn't see his face or anything like that. I can't even describe it. It was like an aura or a gray cloud with white surrounding."

The soul calmed and told Peter he had two young kids who need him and he's not done with life yet.

"You have to go back," it said.

Peter stepped back, and there was a long pause. He says it felt like someone grabbed his arm, but when he turned to look, there was no one there.

"All of a sudden someone opened my eye, and I looked up. At first I thought it was the surgeon but it was someone in the ICU. A nurse or someone like that," says Peter.

"And I woke up in the hospital."

He learned he had flatlined for ten to fifteen-seconds before he was revived. However, doctors hadn't even prepped the electrocardiogram. Peter came back to life on his own.

Reflecting back, Peter is filled with considerable guilt

for wanting to stay on the other side and continue through the doorway, especially given he had a wife and two young children who needed him alive.

"It felt euphoric. I felt the warmth inside me," he says of the white space he visited. "It felt like the most natural thing for me to step over that threshold to go wherever it goes after."

That guilt helps him appreciate the life he has even more now after the near-death experience, he says. But the experience has changed him in other ways as well.

Peter has always had the ability to see and sense things around him that couldn't be seen with the naked eye. He says this has aided him as a paranormal investigator during his many adventures around the globe. He'd taught himself how to ground or switch off that ability so as not to drive himself crazy. After his near-death experience, he had considerable difficulty ignoring that sixth sense.

"The first year and a half (after the near-death experience) I couldn't ground myself. I'd walk into any environment, and I was seeing and I was feeling all kinds of crazy shit," he says. "It got to the point where people were about to say things to me, and I would put words in their mouths straight away. I knew exactly what they were going to say before they said it."

It took Peter the better part of two years to get himself grounded again, and even then he hasn't had the same level of success doing so that he had pre-near-death experience.

He says he doesn't think he ever will. Now, he chooses whether or not he wants to see and feel things from the other side.

"I don't want to be a person who sees shit all the time," says Peter. "I'd rather see it from our side as investigators. The more scientific side."

There's too many people in the history of the human race who've opened themselves up completely to this sixth sense, let anything come through to them, and gone crazy as a result, he says.

The increased psychic ability is something many near-death experiencers mention as a side effect of their experience. In those cases, people claim to have had these abilities all their lives, and standing on death's door amps it up, for lack of a better work. We're going to talk to one such person next.

Like Peter, she's a paranormal investigator who has had strange goings-on in her life from a young age, and these events led her on the path she's on now, exploring haunted locations in and around New York City.

And, like Peter, she found a soul waiting for her on the other side.

CHAPTER SEVEN_
THE MAN IN BLACK

As a medical technician working in the transplant unit of a major New York City hospital, Angela Artuso was no stranger to the concept of death both professionally and personally.

Given the nature of her work, there was always the potential for a patient in her unit to die. It came with the territory and was something she'd become used to, at least as used to as someone can be. Although her overriding desire in any case was for the patients to do well and recover fully.

"You get attached to people, become a part of their family, in a strange sort of way," she says. "But it pretty much overwhelms you."

On a personal level, she'd had strange, unexplainable encounters with death, including her and her husband's relatives. It was these encounters that led her to be a paranormal investigator.

So unlike some of the people we talked to while researching this book, Artuso was already convinced life after death is possible, even probable.

But neither her personal nor professional association with death could prepare her for the day she had a near-death experience. And as is often the case with such profound days, it began typically enough.

She'd woken up on this cold February morning and readied herself for the day, as she did every workday morning. The kids had been sent off to school. Artuso had been dealing with car trouble, so, on this morning, her mother-in-law drove her into work.

Traffic was heavy, so they were unable to take Artuso's usual route in. Her morning packed with meetings and patients coming in for transplants, they decided to drive a different way to the hospital in order to save time.

"I was going over my notes in the car. I had my little notebook out, and I was trying to see what I'd do first before I got there because I knew time was being used up in traffic, so this way I could just dive into it once I got to the hospital," she says.

Confident her mother-in-law would get her to work on time, Artuso paid little attention to the road and traffic around her. But at one point she did look up and out of the vehicle to the left and saw a large truck heading right for them.

"It was on my side. I was sitting in the front passenger's side, and before I could even blink or say anything, the truck just hit us full impact," says Artuso.

The force of impact knocked Artuso's vehicle across the road. The passenger's window exploded in a shower of glass. Given the season, she'd worn a scarf that morning, and as the truck hit and the window shattered, her scarf somehow became tangled in the truck's front grille!

As the vehicles slid across the road in a T shape, the scarf pulled harder and harder around Artuso's throat, she says. She struggled to pull it from her neck, for how long she isn't sure, until it somehow became untangled.

"I'm not sure how. It'd been tied in a knot. But it opened by itself. It didn't tear," she says. "That in itself was bizarre to me."

Everything happened so quickly it's now a blur, she says. Artuso remembers being unable to move, and the whole right side of her body being a mess of blood. At this point all she could do was fight to stay awake and assess the damage she'd been inflicted with.

Her head wasn't injured, but everything else was broken inside her, says Artuso. Looking around, she noticed her mother-in-law was gone. Untouched by the impact, she was able to walk away from the vehicle to get help.

Instead of her mother-in-law, there was a man sitting in the driver's seat. Artuso says he was dressed all in black and had not one flaw on his face, hair, body or clothing.

"His clothing was impeccable. He was dressed all in black. He had on black pants, a black leather jacket and a black shirt," she says. "His hair was the shiniest black hair you'd ever imagine seeing on a person. Almost like glossified shoe polish."

The man's face appeared to be made out of porcelain and his eyes were black, she continues. Whoever he was, he didn't look at Artuso. He looked straight ahead and simply sat in the seat next to her.

Artuso remembers freezing at the sight of him, and thinking, "This is it." She was dying but every fibre of her being told her to stay awake and get out of this car.

"Are you here for me?" she asked the man beside her.

He looked straight ahead and didn't answer.

"So I said again, 'Are you here for me? Is it my time?'"

"No. You're not going anywhere. It's not your time," the man finally responded. "You're not going anywhere. Not yet."

Given most near-death experiencers have described conversations as being telepathic, one would assume the same for Angela. But she says the two actually exchanged spoken words.

The man did not look at her when he spoke either.

Artuso says he looked straight ahead out of the front windshield.

"Almost in like a robotic type of way. He didn't move," she says.

At a loss, all Artuso could do was lie back in her seat and contemplate what was happening to her. She remained like this as the ambulance arrived and paramedics tried to free her from the wreckage. They couldn't, so it was up to firefighters to cut open the vehicle and get her out.

Artuso's injuries were severe enough there was a brief debate about airlifting her to hospital, she says. In the end, the trip was made in an ambulance.

As she lay in the ambulance, struggling to hang on to consciousness, afraid if she fell asleep or passed out, she'd die, she turned to her left, and the Man in Black, as we'll call him, was there with her in the ambulance.

"He was by my side. He was holding my hand and he was holding my arm and he said, 'I have you. I've got you,'" says Artuso.

There was an ambulance technician with her in the cab as well, and she put blankets on Artuso to comfort her. All the while the Man in Black was there, holding her hand and her arm. He told her once more that he had her and that it wasn't her time.

"It's going to be okay," he said to her.

The ambulance arrived at the hospital, pulling up in

front of the Emergency Room. Artuso was pulled from the ambulance toward a waiting bed, and she looked for the Man in Black but couldn't see him anywhere.

"Where's the man? Where's the man who was with me?" she finally asked the gathering of medical staff around her. "I need to talk to him."

"Honey, you were in there by yourself," a doctor said. "The ambulance tech was with you and no one else. That was it. There was no one else."

That moment has stayed with Artuso to this day and left her with many questions. Who was he? What was he? Why was he there? Is he the reason the scarf unraveled from the truck grille, thereby preventing her from being strangled to death? And where did he disappear to?

"Nobody saw him in the car with me. Nobody saw him in the ambulance with me," she says.

Nor did the Man in Black appear again. Not through Artuso's long and painful recovery process in hospital nor the lawsuit that followed the accident. No one bearing his description was called as a witness to the accident. To this day she wonders where he came from and what exactly he was.

"He didn't even really look human," says Artuso.

"You spend your life trying to wrap your head around it, and nothing makes sense. Nothing adds up. I'm still upset talking about it a little bit because it overwhelms me when I do."

The closest Artuso can come to an explanation is the Black-Eyed Children phenomenon. This contemporary series of sightings involved children between the ages of six and sixteen with pale skin and black eyes who are reportedly seen hitchhiking, begging for change, and appearing at people's doorsteps.

There are a couple of key differences though; where the Black-Eyed Children ooze menace and dread, Artuso's Man in Black brought her calm and comfort. And the creatures people have described on the internet and in Reddit threads are unmistakably children, whereas Artuso saw a full-grown man.

"Was he the one who saved my life? I don't know. But he stayed with me and made sure I got the help I needed, and then disappeared into thin air pretty much," she says.

We've already discussed how near-death experiences are subjective, there are commonalities in terms of a bright light and being greeted by a figure or figures, with any communication occurring telepathically.

Artuso's is unique though. There was no light or travelling to a different place. She remained rooted in our world, for lack of a better term. And the being who greeted her spoke to her as any two people would – with his mouth – and the two of them talked back and forth, however briefly.

If these subjective experiences are a result of the experiencer's life, then what in Artuso's existence up to that point could have caused hers to unravel the way it did?

Artuso isn't entirely sure, but hypothesizes her work at the hospital, and dealing with life and death on a daily basis, could've played a part.

She'd been involved in one other accident prior, which took place not long after the birth of her oldest son. She and her husband were out on the town for the first time after the boy was born, and she was hit by a passing vehicle. When Artuso regained consciousness, she was lying beneath the vehicle, a tire resting on her legs.

"That was the only other time (in her life) I could really say I needed a guardian angel on my shoulder, and I had one," says Artuso.

Other than that experience and working in a hospital, Artuso can't think of anything that could have contributed to the Man in Black, she says.

Going back to her near-death experience, Artuso's differs again from others in that she wasn't filled with that euphoric feeling many describe. Had she been, it could've been contributed to the loss of blood she sustained due to her injuries.

Instead, she describes her initial feelings as being shock and disbelief that it had happened. She says everything happened so fast – too fast – and she was at first over-whelmed.

But when she saw the Man in Black, everything changed. She calmed down and came to terms with what was happening, even though she wasn't fully ready for it, hence the battle to stay awake, she says.

"I know I was fully coherent," says Artuso. "I was able to give them (emergency responders) contact information for my husband so they could call him and reach him. So I know I was awake."

Had she been unconscious, or in some semi comatose state, she wouldn't have been able to do that, she says.

Although baffled by the experience, Artuso knows it happened, and she knows she was awake for it.

What's most striking to Artuso, and even to Peter and me after hearing the tale, is the fear she felt during the experience and the struggle to stay awake to prevent herself from dying, which again makes Artuso's experience different from most. The only time hers gels with other experiencers is the peace she eventually felt when her Man in Black assured her this wasn't her time to go, not yet, and the trust she was able to place in that knowledge.

"I pretty much threw my arms up and said, 'It is what it is,' and I just rode with it at that time," says Artuso.

There are many who believe, and the number of people who do is growing, that we each have an angel or spirit guide – or guides even – who look out for us on a daily basis and help us chart our path through life. So was this strange figure a manifestation of Artuso's very own guardian angel?

Artuso says there's been times in her life when there

have been questionable situations, although nothing as traumatic as a near-death experience, where she's felt a presence in her life. Her father passed away at the start of the COVID-19 pandemic, and she remembers getting these feeling, intuitions if you will, that whoever – or whatever – was with her during her death experience was with there again to protect her dad and help her get through his passing.

"There were times that I really felt that extra presence. I couldn't see him, I could not feel him, but I knew it was a man who was by my side, and it got me through it," says Artuso.

"I don't know if the whole situation was bringing me back to that time period and just rehashing it over and over in my mind again, or if whatever was with me that day came back again to help me through the passing of my dad."

Having dedicated a good portion of her life to investigating the paranormal prior to her near-death experience, Peter and I were curious how that whole event changed her view of the paranormal and how she researches and investigates it, if at all?

The experience definitely impacted the way she views life after death and the possibility that ghosts exists among us, she says. There's no doubt in her mind that we continue on after dying in some way, shape, or form.

"There's way more than what we now know," she says.

"And it's not going to be readily accessible for people to accept until they experience it for themselves."

As an investigator, she doesn't impose her beliefs and feelings on others or try to influence them in any way, Artuso says. She believes everyone, whether they are experiencing paranormal activity or not, need to feel it for themselves. As an investigator, it's up to her to adjust her investigations to suit the beliefs of her client.

Her investigations have become a lot more in depth than a simple EVP (electronic voice phenomenon) or Spirit Box session, she says. And she allows herself to feel more and trust her instincts and intuition.

"I don't take things at face value, which is very easy to do in a paranormal investigation. You have to go deeper. You have to dive in deeper," she says.

This includes asking the client if he or she has had a near-death experience, or been exposed to someone who has, and see if that's contributed to the activity they are currently having. She will even ask if they've felt they've been warned about a coming event or received signs to guide them through a difficult time.

"It does change the way you view things, at least in my case it did, but I still try to keep an open mind. For myself, I know there's more," says Artuso.

On a similar topic, Artuso has had a sixth sense, so to speak, and witnessed the spirits of people who have passed on. Anyone who's read Peter and my's previous book, *I*

Want to Believe: An Investigators' Archive, knows of the encounters I speak of. This includes sensing when a spirit is nearby.

Much like Peter, Artuso became much more intuitive after her near-death experience, and like Peter, she didn't know how to filter it. This includes seeing dead people with a greater frequency and hearing the voices of the dead, which she'd never been able to do before.

"I thought I was losing my mind," she says of the frequency and intensity of these encounters.

Artuso turned to a spiritual healer and teacher for help, and she helped her bring this newfound talent, along with her heightened previous ones, under control, she says.

"I'm not a psychic medium. I can't tell you what your future is going to be or what happened here word for word, but I am very empathic," says Artuso.

"I can walk into a room and pick up a feeling immediately. I can sense what other people are feeling without them even talking. All I have to do is look at a picture of them, hear them speak, or just be in the same room as them, and I can pick up the emotion. I can tell what they're going through, and I feel it. I feel it one hundred percent."

She is also able to perform psychometry, or object reading. This allows her to get an impression of a person by holding an object he or she has previously touched. Artuso says she wasn't able to do this prior to her near-death experience.

Artuso still struggles with controlling this talent at times, but she feels she's got a grasp on it most of the time, and this is some two decades later.

There's no doubt in her mind that near-death experiences change the experiencer, and she has a great deal of sympathy for anyone who has one. They leave the experiencer with so much, including a lot of unanswered questions, and you never see life or the world around you the same way.

"It changes you. I can't describe it. Only someone who has been through a traumatic event can understand what someone else whose been through a traumatic event has gone through. Without even saying a word, you know," she says.

Spiritual side aside, the experience also traumatized Artuso at a very human level. She's terrified of trucks to the point where she asks whoever is driving to steer clear of them. And if she is driving, she prefers to have someone else in the vehicle with her.

Even watching a movie where a truck is smashing into or through something upsets her, Artuso says.

"That has been really difficult," she says.

Not all near-death experiences are as traumatic as Artuso's or involved as some of the others we've already discussed, but they nevertheless have a profound impact on the experiencer. We'll travel to the United Kingdom now to discuss one such case.

CHAPTER EIGHT_
A SON'S STORY

Like Angela Artuso, Paul Drake is a paranormal investigator who had long been convinced of life after death prior to having his own near-death experience.

A friend of Peter's, he also hails from the United Kingdom. We chronicled his adventures as a ghost hunter in our last book, *I Want to Believe: An Investigators' Archive* and, at the time, had no idea he'd had a very personal encounter with the other side.

Much like the experience we just discussed, Drake's near-death experience deviates from many we present for you in this book. Compared to such stories, it's almost calming in its presentation, but has had no less of an impact on Drake than Artuso's had on her.

Back in the 1990s, Drake underwent an osteotomy to clear out fluid in one of his legs. Once cleared from the hospital, he returned home and didn't experience any problems for several days.

Then he began to feel pain in the leg one evening, so much so his daughter decided to phone Drake's doctor, who in turn prescribed a pain killer to bring him some relief from the discomfort.

"I didn't know at the time that the medication he put me on, I was allergic to," says Drake.

So Drake unwittingly took his first dose, which he was told to do at night. Surprisingly the pain disappeared instantly. He also quickly realized he had become unaware of what was going on around him. Drake felt relaxed and calm and describes the sensation as being nice.

To hear him tell it, the feeling was not unlike the euphoria many near-death experiencers describe during their time on the other side.

Then his dad appeared before him, which startled Drake, as his father died in 1983!

"And then he disappeared," says Drake. "And in front of me was a garden, and I could feel the air moving. I could feel the grass under my feet."

The garden was surrounded by a fence, and at the opposite end of the garden from Drake there was a gap in the fence. Drake began to walk toward this opening when his dad appeared in front of him once again, blocking his path.

"If you go through this gate, you will not be going back," his dad said, adding the choice was up to Drake.

This gave Drake pause. He's not sure how long he hesitated. It could have been minutes or longer. In the end, he opted not to cross through the opening, and his father told him he'd made the right choice.

"It's not your time yet, son," his father said.

What his father said, and how he said it, was out of line with the man's character. Drake says his dad never spoke to him that way while he was alive. We'll get to more on that shortly.

Drake's wife watched while all this was happening. He was seated, oblivious to what was going on around him. She'd try talking to him, but he was unresponsive. So she yelled and even resorted to hitting him about the face, hoping to shock him back to reality, he says.

"My wife said I was looking at her, but not at her at the same time," says Drake, indicating his eyes were open the whole time. "She could see me talking to somebody."

He slowly came back to life, and his wife could see her husband talking to somebody, but there was nobody else there, says Drake. When he was fully conscious, she told Drake he was having a full-on conversation with someone, and he told her he was talking with his dad.

Drake had an allergic reaction to the medication and was told never to take it again. He was checked out by his doctor, who when all was said and done, filed the incident as a near-death experience, as well as an allergic reaction to painkillers.

What sticks with Drake after all this time is how real the experience felt, right down to the sensation of the grass beneath his feet and the breeze on his face, he says.

"I could hear the birds singing. The grass was dry and waving in the wind. It was just so real," says Drake.

"I sometimes wonder to myself, 'Should I have gone through that fence?'"

That statement harkens back to Peter's experience, where he felt a definite pull to continue on to whatever waits on the other side of the gateway. It's interesting that, in Drake's case, he found himself in a garden instead of a corridor or a bright, white space. He says the garden didn't represent any he'd ever seen, at least not one he consciously remembers.

"It was like you're walking down the country lane and you see this garden. I stopped to look at this garden, and I could see a fence and the gate. The gate wasn't there, and I wanted to go through and see what was on the other side," he says.

"But I couldn't see over the fence. I couldn't see what was there."

There was no anxiety. Drake says he felt like the garden was exactly where he was meant to be at that time.

"I was calm. I was relaxed," says Drake.

But there was a sensation he has a hard time putting

words to, and it has to do with the gateway and passing through it. He says he felt like a kid wanting to do something but knowing his parents wouldn't approve of it.

"Should I put my finger in the light socket? Things like that," Drake says.

Having his father appear before him and stop him, as any attentive parent would, stuck with Drake for years after the fact. Describing that moment now, the emotion that crosses his face is hard to ignore.

Drake never got along with his father while his parent was alive, largely because the man was absent for the better part of the young Drake's life. His dad worked Monday to Friday and would be off to work before Drake woke up for school, he says. And his father didn't get home at night until just before Drake was going to bed.

"So I didn't see him very often at all," he says.

On Friday nights his dad would go to the pub after work, as is the custom with many hard working Englishmen. Dad also embarked for the pub Saturdays at lunch time and Sundays for dinner and didn't often return until late, says Drake. In short, the son rarely saw his father.

"He died when I was twenty-two," says Drake. "So over that time I probably saw him a year in total."

Money was tight in those days, so the family didn't go on a lot of holidays, he says, adding it was hard to feel any kind of connection with the man while he was alive.

Peter echoes Drake's experience with a similar story of

his own, saying his parents didn't have a lot of money either, so family life involved sitting and eating in front of the TV while having a drink and a smoke. This routine was broken up, for his father at least, by visits to the local pub. Such was the way for many English families during the 1970s and 1980s.

And rarely, if ever, would a father tell his child he loved him or her, says Peter.

"It was like this brick wall," Peter says.

Drake says it took him a good twenty-two years to come to terms with his father's death. He never talked about it with anyone. His mother withdrew from most around her afterward, and he felt there was no one to turn to. Eventually, Drake spoke with a counsellor about his father and his passing, and was able to make sense of it.

He adds the near-death experience, which occurred at around the same time he was wrapping up his counselling, helped him get the closure he needed.

"It was like he was saying, 'bye Paul,'" says Drake.

Although Drake didn't respect the man while he was alive, he has a renewed respect for him now, and he believes his dad prevented him from walking through the gateway into a premature death. Given his research into the paranormal, he hopes the two will somehow cross paths again one day, he says.

"The fact that he stopped me, or advised that I didn't

go further (through the gate), I know that was him. That was my dad," says Drake.

"Seeing my dad was a life changer, pure and simple."

Drake witnessed a spirit before his near-death experience. He was a delivery driver dropping off an order at a pub early one day, and witnessed a ghostly patron known to staff who worked there. But seeing his dad brought the whole concept of life after death into focus for him, he says.

As is the case with every near-death experiencer, Drake's view of life changed dramatically after his recovery. Prior to that day, Drake describes himself as not a confident person. If there was a problem, he walked away from it. If there was a confrontation to be had, he'd try to avoid it, even if it was for the better.

He decided that needed to change, and he'd make the most of life from that moment forward. Drake still doesn't like to argue or push a point, but he'll do it.

"It made me realize that I've got a life to live, and I decided I was going to live it," he says.

The experience also made him more of a spiritual person. Drake describes himself as a spiritualist – a person who believes spirits of the dead exist and have the ability and desire to communicate with the living – and attended meetings with psychics and mediums in hope of talking with his father again.

Such an encounter has yet to happen, he says.

His view of religion has also changed. He never considered himself religious before, nor does he subscribe to a particular religion now, but he does believe in Christianity and Spiritualism, the latter in particular because it presented itself to him.

Like Peter and Artuso, Drake now sees spirits around him with frequency, and like Peter and Artuso, he tries to keep a handle on that gift as much as possible, especially when investigating the paranormal. He'd prefer the clients he helps experience a ghostly encounter for themselves so they can get the validation they need, he says.

When it comes to the traditional belief in God, however, Drake isn't sure.

"I do believe there's something there, there's something that worked on us," he says. "Whether you call him God or what you like, I don't know."

Having had a father die early in life myself, I sympathize with Drake and his story. It took me the better part of thirty years to come to terms with my dad's passing, and I know my journey into the paranormal helped me find peace. Was Drake's near-death experience born out of a desire to finally get some closure? Is there a correlation between experiencing trauma and believing there's more to life than what we see on the surface, as Jolene Lindsey suggests? I believe so, although there's still more to it than that.

Peter and I interviewed many experiencers during the

course of researching this book, and there's many of their stories left to tell. But we're going to take a break from the storytelling and return to the realm of science for a moment, because there are some scientists and researchers taking a serious look at the near-death phenomenon. One such man is Andrea Soddu.

CHAPTER NINE_
NUMBERS AND WORDS

TRADITIONAL SCIENTIFIC AND ACADEMIC RESEARCH into the near-death phenomenon is conducted using standardized questionnaires like the Greyson Scale. Interviewees are asked questions like "Did you feel separated from your body?" or "Did you have a feeling of peace?" in order to get a sense of what the experience was like.

This approach has been largely criticized, with those critics saying it creates a bias that can skew one's recollection of events and therefore subsequent discoveries.

But a recent study of near-death experiences by members of Western University and University of Liege broke with tradition and used text mining and artificial intelligence to explore the phenomenon. This provided an opportunity to use an unbiased approach and come to a scientific conclusion.

Researchers investigated one hundred and fifty-eight

participants by analyzing text narratives of experiencers following their near-death experience. By using this technique, called text mining, the scientists could perform an unbiased evaluation, says Andrea Soddu, a member of Western University's Brain and Mind Institute.

It also provided valuable and measurable data like the frequency and correlation of key words like "see," "light," "dead," and "fear," he says.

Before we continue with what Soddu and his colleague discovered, and why it's important to near-death research, let's answer the obvious questions: why Soddu and why he wanted to explore near-death experiences.

Much like Lawrence Ward, whom we learned about a few chapters ago, Soddu is fascinated by consciousness. Prior to being a professor at Western University in London, Ontario, Canada, he was part of the Coma Science Group with pioneering neurologist Steven Laureys. There, his expertise in functional MRI (magnetic resonance imaging) was used to explore brain activity in patients who'd been in a coma.

"Some times, after going to coma, they'd wake up with disabilities but their consciousness is intact. Some of the time they wake up in what is called a vegetative state so they are awake, they show the sleep/waking cycle, but they are completely unaware," says Soddu.

"What we try to do is see if there is any residual sign of consciousness."

As Ward discovered, vegetative patients do show levels of consciousness. And Soddu believes there are striking similarities between this state and the near-death experience. So it wasn't much of a leap for him to turn his attention to the aforementioned study, which was conducted in late 2019, and the results of which were made public in early 2020.

Soddu and Laureys are fascinated by consciousness and any change in perception, he says. They believe a near-death experience causes an abrupt change in perception caused by what he calls a "cascade of events" that transpires when one is faced with such a trauma. This trauma can be triggered by coma, electrocution, and a variety of other potentially fatal situations.

"We believe there is a strong change in perception in the way that we perceive ourselves and the external world," says Soddu.

Putting this theory to the test, Soddu and his colleagues in Belgium started compiling data from near-death experiences both in Canada and abroad. First-person near-death accounts were written down in an essay format. Soddu says these were written freely with no guidelines. The experiencer could recount his or her experience however they felt most comfortable.

"Just describe whatever you remember about your near-death experience," he told them.

"There was no limitation at all."

Soddu says the Greyson Scale was used after the fact in order to measure whether or not the accounts would be classified as a near-death experience or not. This was done only to establish a baseline for the phenomenon, but not to influence what researchers were told.

Once the texts were collected, researchers looked for the frequency of repeated words like "light" and "light tunnel," "well-being," "death," "body" and many others. Soddu says this is the first analysis the team did, and they found some thirty words were repeated with frequency.

"Light" was repeated the most, with the word turning up in one hundred and six accounts, or sixty-seven percent of the cases, he says. "Tunnel" was found in fifty-five of the documented cases, or thirty-five percent of the time.

I found this most interesting because it seems the majority of near-death experiences we hear about in popular culture involve a tunnel of light. Clearly, at least according to this study, that is not the case.

Once the researchers completed this stage of the study, they looked to see if these words were in any way related or not, says Soddu. This was done by taking words like "tunnel" and "light" and seeing if they turned up together in individual accounts.

"Then you can calculate substantially what is called the distance between these two words," he says.

If words like "light" and "tunnel" are present in all the documented cases, there is substantially no distance between them, says Soddu. If a word is present in one account but not in any other, there is a great distance between them. The neuroscientists then developed visual representations like graphs and dendrograms to illustrate the proximity of these words as they relate to positive and negative connotations about near-death experiences.

What Soddu and company learned was positive-toned words like "see" and "light" turned up with greater frequency than negative words like "fear" and "death," as these words had a greater distance between them, he says.

"It looks like the experiences these people have are not only positive. There is a mixture of positive and negative experiences, but the nice thing is, when you look at the words that connote a negative experience and the words that connote a positive experience, they come in clusters," Soddu says.

When these clusters were analyzed, there were fewer negative words in a cluster than positive. This is important because it suggests people do not view their near-death experience as negative, says Soddu.

"Words like 'light' and 'well' tended to be more frequent," he says.

The word "dead" appeared in eighteen percent of documented cases, and "fear" turned up in twenty-four percent of them. Although there were both positive and negative words used, when analyzed these words did not appear together in clusters, but remained separate.

What's interesting is how these conclusions are in line with everything we've learned so far about near-death experiences. Even the most traumatic ones, like Artuso's and even Taylor's, have a positive effect on the experiencer. They achieve a new outlook and appreciation for life, are given greater insight into the world around them, or resolve some piece of unfinished business, much like Drake did in the last chapter.

Soddu's findings also support the notion each near-death experience is subjective, yet has commonalities. In many cases there's a tunnel and there's a light, but not always a tunnel of light. I was compelled to ask the professor why he thought this was. Is this a case of people hearing about near-death experiences, having one of their own, and their mind filling in the blanks? Or are these experiences just similar enough?

"I think there is a cultural bias," says Soddu. "In fact, I think it would be interesting to study near-death experience in a population where they don't know about the literature. They don't know about the novels that describe the near-death experience."

With that cultural bias out of the equation, Soddu would be interested to see if words like "tunnel" and "light" show up in documented cases, he says.

So what's Soddu's take away from all this? Did he believe in near-death experiences prior to engaging in the study? As a matter of fact, he did.

"I believe in the terminology of the near-death experience. I do believe in out-of-body experience. I do believe in the historic perception of the word," says Soddu.

To explain further, Soddu recounts the story of a friend who is a paramedic. In his spare time, this friend likes to create art and he was using electricity to create patterns in wood for a project, says Soddu, adding his friend was being very cavalier in his use of the electricity.

"You can use electricity to draw patterns on wood," he says. "You use high voltage, and the current creates its own pattern on the surface of the wood, and it burns it at the same time."

There was an electrical arc and his paramedic friend was electrocuted, Soddu says. At first, another friend who was video taping the project thought the paramedic was joking, mimicking the actions of someone being electrocuted. Fortunately, this friend clued in that what was happening was real and called out to his wife for help. She is a nurse and was able to treat the paramedic until an ambulance arrived.

Soddu says it took two cardiac shocks to bring his friend back to life. By then, more than eleven minutes had passed.

His friend is not a religious person, but a spiritual person. He described to Soddu a sense of peace and belonging in a place void of stress and need. All sense of time was gone, and there was no Ego in the sense of there being no needs, wants or desires.

Pain only entered into the equation when he felt the second electric shock that brought his friend back to life, he says.

"He describes his experience as the most beautiful he ever had," says Soddu. "It was a very, very positive experience."

Interestingly enough, the paramedic told Soddu he was literally able to smell his own body after he woke up. Not like when one is sweating after a workout, but because he was back in it. And that made him very uncomfortable.

"He felt like he was brought back to being human or being alive, and it was something that he didn't feel comfortable with at the very beginning," says Soddu.

The friend accepted the fact he was alive, but his view of the world had changed. Soddu says this is much like someone having undergone some kind of therapy or treatment.

"It's something that is long lasting. It's not like it's there for just a moment," he says. "It's really changing the way you see things."

Soddu wonders if this change in point of view is the person rationally adapting to what has happened, or if something happened in the brain that rewired the person's perception of things?

He is also hesitant to say if his research supports the

notion of life after death or not. In the end, he says the research doesn't support an answer one way or the other.

"Substantially we're measuring the terminology because the language is powerful. Sometimes we forget that. It's so rich and can tell you a lot," says Soddu.

"Just looking at the way they (the experiencers) write an essay, the words they use and how the words are phrased, it can tell a lot about the experience and what they see."

What is clear to Soddu is people who go through a near-death experience are transformed in some way, which proves to him that something is happening in their brain that's for the better.

"If they can, in that moment, experience what turns out to be an afterlife, well, then they are definitely having that experience," he says. "If they are religious, then they definitely confirmed that position. If they are spiritual, they may feel like this sense of consciousness, which is everywhere. This is powerful."

The moment that you feel like you belong to something, you feel protected, says Soddu. You are not lost.

Even if near-death experiences are something that can't yet be scientifically understood, there is still a sense of comprehension that goes beyond what is science, says Soddu. And even if science can't answer all the questions behind these experiences, there's still an understanding that goes beyond rationality.

"That's powerful," says Soddu.

I find Soddu's scientifically open mind to be a powerful thing, as is his willingness to not discount the experiences people have because he and other scientists can't provide all the answers. Nor can they discount what people are experiencing. It's clear to him, and to Peter and me, that something is happening to people that's beyond our current knowledge and understanding of life and death.

Which means it's time to hear another story from one who believes they've touched the other side.

CHAPTER TEN_
SEEING THE WORLD AS IT TRULY IS

When Peter Panagore died and came back to life, he was completely unaware that what he'd experienced was part of a larger phenomenon.

In fact, he spent decades keeping his near-death experience a secret out of fear he'd be ridiculed or looked at as crazy.

"Because it sounded crazy when I said it out loud," says Panagore. "But I knew the reality of it was the truth of my entire existence."

He describes those years after dying as living in two worlds: an interior world and an exterior world. And the interior world bled into the exterior with what he describes as eccentricities that come from understanding the essence of being was the impermanence of life.

"I couldn't hide that stuff, but I never told anybody why I was that way," he says.

Panagore was a born natural mystic prior to his near-death experience. He had an out-of-body/angelic experience when he was five, and then again when he was six. Each time he came away a different person than he was before, he says.

The first time, he came back with an understanding he had a task in life that was much bigger than himself, which is a heady understanding to have when you're just five years old, says Panagore.

"The deal had been made long before I'd been born," he says.

The second experience was equally mind blowing, as Panagore claims he witnessed infinity while in human form, a concept that is still hard to put into words.

While in high school he took a triple hit of mescaline, a psychedelic drug known for its hallucinatory properties, and had an experience he describes as feeling the living presence of the Divine within the living world. Soon after, Panagore, who attended a Catholic high school, began practicing a centering meditation and prayer in order to commune with this divine presence.

Continuing his mystical ways in college, he experienced two more out-of-body experiences while hiking the Appalachian trail in the Eastern United States, encountering the same angelic form he'd witnessed as a boy.

"Two things came out of that, so far as I understand anyway. I was going to be given a gift that I'd have to give away and that I would not be consumed by Divine Fire, even though it would feel like that's exactly what was happening, especially after my NDE," he says.

How did all these experiences affect young Panagore? He'd spoken with his parents not long before our interview, and they'd told him he was atypical in his compassion as a child. This was after his out-of-body experiences at five and six years of age, he says. He lost some of that while growing up, but it returned after the mescaline trip during his senior year at high school.

"It popped right open, and from then on I was on the path," says Panagore. "But I had no idea what any of this meant. No idea. It's only in hindsight that I understand any of it."

While each of these experiences were earth-shattering to Panagore, they wouldn't be put in context until a year after his college trip to the Appalachians. Panagore was ice climbing in Mount Assiniboine Provincial Park along the Alberta-British Columbia border in Canada. Panagore spent eight days back-country skiing and snow caving with another outdoor enthusiast and having the vacation of a lifetime.

When it came to the eventual ice climb, Panagore made a miscalculation and climbed with an ax and a hammer instead of two axes. He'd been in the mountains all his life, but those climbs couldn't prepare him for a winter ascent in the Canadian Rockies.

"That kind of messed me up. It slowed me down," he says, reflecting back.

This led to a long night of surviving death on the side of a snowy mountain in temperatures that have killed many a careless climber and unprepared outdoor adventurer. Panagore says it was during his rappel in an effort to get off the mountain that hypothermia finally took him. His final thoughts before blacking out were of his parents.

"When I died, my consciousness stayed awake," he says. "I was not understanding what was going on. I wasn't scared, but I was confused."

Panagore could still see, yet all he could see was darkness. He didn't know he was dead but thought he'd fallen asleep, as he'd been struggling to stay awake through the hypothermia. Every time he had fallen asleep due to the hypothermia, he'd lost consciousness, but not this time.

This time was different, says Panagore. This time the darkness in front of him became enormous. It actually had a visible depth to it. Then, far in the distance, there appeared a pinprick of light, which rushed toward him.

"I'd describe it as intelligence. Hyper intelligence. Super intelligence. And it rushed toward me faster than the speed of light from an incredibly far distance," says Panagore.

As it came to him, the light grew in size and communicated with him telepathically. Panagore clarifies too that he didn't hear words in his head, but understood what was about to happen. He says the light intended to take him to the other side, which he resisted.

"I don't know what's going on here, but I'm not going anywhere," he remembers thinking.

What Panagore resisted the most was how powerful and intelligent the light was. He says it was all-powerful and all-knowing, and that was intimidating.

He also noted this experience was different from his previous out-of-body experiences because this was the first time he felt a sense of leaving his body, says Panagore. The previous times he ended up outside his body without any sense of happening. Previously, he still felt connected to his body, but not this time. He felt separation.

"This time was like 'it's over,'" he says.

Despite his resistance, the light took him and returned to its point of origin at the same speed it rushed to Panagore. And Panagore was within this being, but had an astral body of his own that he was aware of. He says he knew this being of light as well, as he identified it as the same entity that had been picking him up all along during his previous experiences.

The entity continued to speak to him telepathically and expressed words of love and comfort the entire time, he says. It took him into a void that was both dark and illuminated at once, and Panagore was able to see in every direction. He describes it as being able to see deep into infinity, but not to the origin of infinity.

"It's full of paradox, and I can only talk about it in metaphor," he says. "I'm in this place, and I'm no longer a thing. I'm in no-thing ness. I'm in nothingness. There are no things there, and I am not a thing. I'm an orb or energy. I'm a consciousness that is independent and also comfortable. I was not afraid."

For the first time in his life, Panagore recognized who and what he really was, and his brain was no longer inhibited in its thinking. He says there was no delay in his thought process, and anything and everything he needed to know was there.

This is consistent with other experiencers as they have described knowing everything they needed to know in a single, simple thought. This includes reaching into the past for information or a memory, and even being able to do the same for events in the future that haven't happened yet.

Some experiencers have been told when loved ones were going to die and, upon returning to life, suffered these deaths of family members. This is what happened to Mary Neal, an orthopedic surgeon who drowned after a kayaking accident in Chile. She lay submerged at the bottom of a waterfall deprived of oxygen for twenty-four minutes. During that time, beings told her about the future death of her oldest son, and ten years later, it happened.

Panagore admits this all sounds crazy, and that's why he didn't discuss his experience for years, which is the case with many near-death experiencers. He learned this lesson after talking about his first out-of-body experience and receiving a chilly reception from everyone he tried discussing it with.

He continues, saying a portal opened before him, and a liquid flow of energy emerged, which was transparent and solid all at once. This energy was instantly attractive to him, and he reached out with his being and touched it. The energy, in turn, flowed into him and expanded him like a balloon.

As this happened, Panagore went through what he describes as a "hell of my own making through life" where he experienced every negative emotion he'd ever felt and every negative experience he put others through. He says this was done through the perspective of every person he'd ever hurt. At the same time, he went through every rationale he thought up in the moment for behaving this way.

"I knew I created this. I was being shown this. It wasn't something that was hidden," he says. "There are no hidden parts to me. I am naked before the Divine. There's no place to hide and I see all this suffering."

All the while, this voice – the Voice – of creation spoke to him, telling him it created him and showed him his own creation. Panagore says he saw the length of his soul, witnessed his previous lives, which were all happening simultaneously.

His past lives were but a pebble in an ocean compared

to the size of his soul, and his soul was the same when compared to the divine light he was in, says Panagore.

Panagore was then shown the existence of humanity, which he describes as being within a "matrix of software" that is designed in such a way that humanity, and all of your universe, can exist, and the only way it can exist is to be flawed.

"Everything in (humanity) is flawed. There is all flaw inside of it. Flaw for me is seeing the pain I'd caused others, and I could see that everyone caused pain to everyone else, and everything in the whole world, the whole universe, consumed everything else," he says.

"It wasn't my fault that I'd done these things. It was the nature of my being human."

This life review, which Panagore judged himself guilty by taking ownership of all the bad things he'd done, is similar to what Scott Taylor described in his chapter.

The Voice then told Panagore he was forgiven and loved, and that it – the Divine Light – had always known and loved him. Despite his flaws, he was loved. Panagore says he turned his heart from the sadness he felt at the pain he'd caused others toward this love, and was expanded even larger by it.

"All of my suffering, all of my karma, all of my sins, everything that was flawed of myself fell away with myself," says Panagore. "I was no longer myself. Peter was no longer in existence. I was this one created consciousness that was made from the Creator, and I was in-filled with beauty, love, light, awe."

All of this endless hope, knowledge, wisdom, and reason was one thing – one giant love so enormous it was without end, he says. This existed outside and inside him as he kept expanding.

Then he began contracting back to his previous soul self, and with that came memories. Memories of his parents, of his sister who had run away from home when Panagore was fourteen. He says this broke his family for decades and was indeed the reason Panagore had taken on these grueling outdoor adventures.

"When someone vanishes from your life, it's like a death only there's no burial, there's no memorial. There's emptiness and unhappiness," says Panagore.

He asked the Divine if he was dead, and the answer was yes. He continued, saying he could not die now because it would destroy his parents if they lost another child.

At this, Panagore was carried across what he can only describe as Heaven to some kind of boundary, which he was thrust through, he says. On the other side he witnessed an endless expanse of stars and galaxies before his focus was narrowed down to one galaxy, then our solar system, and then Earth itself, which appeared as a type of hologram.

And on this hologram, Panagore claims he saw every

living person on Earth existing in real time all at once. Within each of them existed a golden fleck of light, which he understood to be the eternal nature of love.

Covering this holographic depiction of Earth and its peoples was a foam, he says. This foam prevented others from seeing this love within them and everyone else.

"In the way that I love you now, I have always loved you," this divine entity told Panagore. At this, he understood this same thing was true of every human being.

Panagore understood then that he was unique, but so was everyone else. Within that uniqueness was an equality we all share, he says.

Zooming up from the Earth were the faces of his parents, and he saw the suffering they would endure without him in real time, says Panagore. This suffering would continue until their deaths.

However, at the same time, he saw his parents' lives and the love they would all share were he still alive. At that he realized his life – everyone's physical lives – is but a wink in the existence of time.

"Stay," the Divine entity said to him then. "You see their suffering will end in the wink of an eye and they'll be here and free. Stay here. You don't have to go back."

All Panagore could see was his parents' suffering, he says. He knew then he had more life left to live.

"I haven't gone all the way into you yet," he told the

light around him. "There's still some of me left here. Do I have to go?"

"We want you to come," the Voice replies.

A debate ensued, with Panagore insisting he wasn't ready to go, but that he'd one day like to return to this place he was currently in, he says. The Divine entity told him he could.

"Then I choose to live my life," he said.

"You won't live your life," was the response.

At that, Panagore describes being "flicked" like a bug backwards. As he fell back, he became denser and thicker. All around him were these portals and the voice of the Divine said to him, "Choose."

"And I know I have to choose an entry point back into my body. Like I have all these lives that I could live, and I could pick any one of them," says Panagore.

This part of Panagore's story hit home for me, as it was strikingly similar to the experience I had that long night back in 2018. Had I, in some way, found myself in the same realm as Panagore had? If so, how and why? How many people have this experience, and what happens if you choose a different path back to life?

A laser beam of light was presented to Panagore, and he was again encouraged to enter it, but he decided not to, he says. Instead, he chose to have a measure of autonomy – selfishness if you will – by returning to some version of his life.

He picked a portal on the fringe of this light, just on the cusp of its full radiance, he says. Within this portal he saw all the possibilities his life still had in store for him. These were things he could choose to do, others could choose for him, or were left up to fate itself.

Pausing for a moment, which I appreciate, as my brain is still processing the last bits of his story and how they relate to my experience, Panagore explains he now lives in a constant state of déjà vu. He says he's constantly seeing the world unfold right before it happens, and this occurs all the time.

This sounds almost like the kind of awareness Peter and Artuso describe. Many experiencers also claim to live in a state of déjà vu or some form of heightened awareness after their experience.

Personally, I have frequently experienced déjà vu and increased empathy since that night in 2018. I've also had prophetic dreams and dreamt about what can best be described as past lives... but more on that in a future chapter.

Panagore says this déjà vu was incredibly disruptive for the longest time after his experience. In the end, he had to get used to it and better understand it in order to live comfortably.

The journey through that tunnel felt like being crushed down from being an ocean to the size of a pebble, he says.

"It felt like I was being corkscrewed back into this body and I was being done to. I had no choice in this. This is all being done to me," says Panagore.

His brain coming back online was instant suffering, he says. There was pain everywhere. Panagore's feet, hands and eyeballs were frozen, which made sense given where he and his climbing partner were. But the entirety of his physical being hurt. It hurt to be alive again.

"The worst pain of my life, my re-entry into this world," he says.

Worst of all, Panagore understood he was not the body he wore but a being of light and love connected to something bigger than mere existence. To be back in a physical form again, that was pain and suffering to him. At first, he couldn't remember how to speak, nor did he understand what his climbing partner was screaming at him while he was shaken awake.

As he was hauled to his feet, Panagore had no recollection of who or where he was. Nor did he know the man who was yelling at him, telling him he'd died and that, if Panagore had died, he'd have died too.

It turns out the two men had been stuck in this place on the mountain for hours. With Panagore awake, they made a final descent to the bottom and self-treated for hypothermia in their tent, he says. Once they were warm enough, the two got in their vehicle and drove to the nearest town.

By now, Panagore was aware of what happened and who he was, but things had changed. He uses the Keanu Reeves movie The Matrix as an example. He knew this world wasn't real he says. He could now "see the code" of its design, but he didn't know what to do with it.

He describes seeing radiant light inside every living thing, and this light spoke silently of love and unity. Panagore says every living thing is called into being as a soul using an unpronounceable name, at least unpronounceable by human language.

All this he can hear inside him all the time, he says.

"All I knew was my entire inner perspective had shifted, and I could see what no one else could," says Panagore. "And I knew they couldn't see it, and I knew if I told them about it, they still wouldn't be able to see it."

As the days passed and Panagore spent more time alive, he realized how ugly everything seemed on the surface, at least to him and his new perspective on life. Not like from a horror movie but simply crude and broken and less than what was intended.

On the inside was a roaring light of sound that encouraged him to speak, but he didn't know how or about what to speak, he says.

Again, as you've already read and will continue to read throughout this book, Panagore's post near-death experience is not unlike others. He came back different, changed even, and saw the world in a new light. He understood there was more to life than what the majority of us view on the surface, and he knew his existence had changed forever.

This holds true for myself as well, even though I can't see how my experience was near death at all.

Having grown up Catholic, I wondered how Panagore's near-death experience changed his perspective on religion. He says everything he'd been taught and told growing up no longer applied.

Religion is something humans made up in order to make sense of these strange, paranormal experiences people were having, he says. If what he met on the other side was indeed God, and the place he'd gone was Heaven, then religion wasn't needed.

"Everything about humanity, everything we've ever done, the words we use, the cultures we make, the societies we've built, is all frickin' made up. All of it. It's come right out of our heads," says Panagore.

"It has no reality for me."

For our interview, which was done virtually, Panagore dressed in a dress shirt in order to make himself presentable, as one does for such an occasion. He says he had to teach himself to do this in order to fit into the society in which he lives.

When he travels to other countries, he does his best to not stand out, he says. He blends into the local culture as best he can.

"I do that right where I live in New England," says Panagore. "I'm incredibly eccentric, and I don't need to present that way."

His mystical experiences didn't stop with that near-death experience. Panagore had several more over the years that helped heal him and adjust to life on this plane of existence. He also suffered a heart attack in 2015 and briefly died.

He says this second near-death experience made him "all in" and open to talking about these experiences without fear of ridicule.

You know it's a mystical experience because you come out of it not the same person as you were before, says Panagore, who initially feared being consumed, for lack of a better word, by the Divine entity. But each mystical experience was another opportunity to "get on board," so to speak with the reality of our existence. And each one he had broke down this resistance until he accepted his fate.

Panagore now writes and speaks about his experiences. Instead of going into architecture, he's what he describes his life long ministry as a "trouble making social worker with a gift for healing, helping, and speaking." He worked in television for fifteen years as well, where he talked openly about his experiences.

About half of the world's population have had a mystical experience, but these are repressed because people are afraid to talk about them for fear of how others will react. And tens of millions of people have had near-death experiences all over the world and came back knowing religion doesn't exist, and even those who stay within their religion have a very different, very mystical perspective on it.

"The near-death community, I think, is a vocal expression of the Divine nature of all life in such numbers that have never lived on Earth before," says Panagore.

The light people find inside themselves, and see in others, after their near-death experience speaks to itself and to each other. As people who have had these experiences begin to openly talk about them, and to each other, it magnifies this Divine Light. Panagore believes this is the beginning of a spiritual awakening of sorts for people on this planet or, as he sees it, plane of existence.

"This is just the beginning. Sixty years since cardiac care came along. Tens of millions of us in the United States alone. Multiplied all over the world wherever there's modern medical technology, which is pretty much everywhere," says Panagore.

"There's this universalism of humanity that no matter who we are, or where we are, it's a chance for this planet for the first time."

As far as Panagore is concerned, this is about one planet, one being, because the Divine Light is within all living things.

Panagore's experiences and the beliefs born from them

are inspiring in their own way. He sees the human Ego as the creator behind religion and society and all the rules and regulations that go with it. If people can let go of the Ego, and embrace who they are, he believes humanity, and the world, will be a better place.

Even if you don't believe everything that happened to him – as it is quite a story he tells, one I find compelling – the message of hope Panagore came back with is one I can get on board with. Hopefully, having read it, others will too.

Let's move on to another person's experience, one that differs from the rest because it happened to the experiencer while she was a child.

CHAPTER ELEVEN_
RAINBOWS AND SONG

When Marlene Cassidy was little, she spent a lot of time in Girl Guides and Pathfinders, which afforded the young city girl plenty of opportunities for adventure and companionship.

Cassidy grew up in Surrey, British Columbia, Canada, which is essentially a suburb of Vancouver, the largest city in Western Canada. At the time, Surrey was primarily ranch and farmland, a far cry from the busy commercial and residential center it is today.

Still, fifteen-year-old her looked forward to attending the summer Guide camps as the events took her into the heartland of the province and away from the hustle and bustle of where she lived.

This one summer found Cassidy and a small group of girls at a camp in Chilliwack, an agricultural community about sixty-three miles east of Vancouver. As an outing,

Cassidy's Guide leader took the girls to nearby Cultus Lake for a day of swimming and water adventure with other youth groups.

Cassidy remembers the setting well, with its beaches and long docks stretching out into the lake. Everyone was having fun in the sun, and the plan was to spend a good couple of hours there.

A lot of the girls lay on one of the docks, suntanning, and Cassidy was one of them. Not being able to swim, she had no intention of going any closer to the water.

Then a couple of the older kids began pitching girls off the dock and into the lake, and they drew closer to Cassidy, who grew increasingly nervous.

"I got up because I wanted to leave. I didn't want to go in the water," she says, reflecting back.

Two of the girls got hold of her before she could reach the beach, and began heaving her to and fro, intent on tossing her into the lake. Cassidy says her panic increased.

"No, no no!" she screamed at them. "I can't swim."

Too late. The girls tossed young Cassidy into the lake.

Cassidy was small for her age, and the girls were able to throw her quite far out into the water. She remembers hitting the surface and hearing the girls' laughter before sinking into the depths.

People who almost drown claim they are unable to make any noise nor cry for help. They are too busy trying to keep their heads above water. Cassidy says this was true for her. All her energy went into trying to stay afloat. She couldn't even lift her hand above her head to signal for help. And every time she opened her mouth to yell, it filled with water.

"And I was too busy trying to take a breath," she says.

It quickly became clear to her that no one was paying attention to what was going on. No one rushed out to save her. In fact, it appeared she'd been totally forgotten.

"I think they thought I was joking about not being able to swim," says Cassidy.

She soon felt the weeds at the bottom of the lake touch her toes and realized she was a long way from the surface. Cassidy looked up, and the sunlight on the surface had filtered out and dimmed all around her.

Floating on the bottom of the lake, a strange calmness came over Cassidy, she says. She tried to walk along the bottom back to shore but couldn't gain any traction. She soon accepted she was going to drown.

"That's when all of a sudden there were these colors all through the water," says Cassidy. "And I watched these colors move through the water like a wave and come towards me."

There was every color of the rainbow moving toward her, and accompanying it was music. Cassidy says it was music like she'd never heard music before. It was neither singing nor instrumental, yet, at the same time, it was.

"It sounded otherworldly. I've never heard music like

that before in my life, and I've never really heard it since," she says. "It was indescribable."

With the wave of music came an increased sense of calm, she says. Cassidy could also feel the warmth of the sun even though she was deep under the water. It felt like she was down there forever, but it might have only been for a few minutes.

Cassidy took a breath, sucking in a bunch of water, and was then yanked out of the lake by a pair of hands. There was a burst of pain, as her lungs were full of water. She remembers the sensation of being hauled up onto the dock, her torso and legs scratching across the rough material as she was then placed on the surface.

Her eyes popped open, and several panicked faces looked down at her, the group having realized too late that Cassidy really couldn't swim. Cassidy says she coughed up an unknown amount of water, and her body felt heavy from the ordeal.

She also felt sad. Cassidy says the experience with the lights and music was so beautiful that she didn't want it to end. Now she was lying on this dock with a bunch of strangers looking at her and touching her, and she was in pain. She wished she was back in the water again.

Cassidy's mother was informed about what had happened, and she was understandably upset. What made the situation worse was Cassidy's father had died just two years prior, adding extra trauma to what happened.

The young Cassidy apologized, saying she shouldn't have been on the dock to begin with.

"She put me in swimming lesson nonetheless," says Cassidy.

Something her mom said next has stuck with Cassidy until this very day: "This makes me think so much of your dad when he almost drowned," her mom said.

Cassidy had never heard about this before. "Dad almost drowned?" she replied.

At this point, she had told her mom nothing about what happened while she was in the water. Cassidy says she was unsure about what actually happened, and didn't want to bring it up.

"Was it from lack of oxygen or things going off in my head?" she wondered. "I was fifteen. I wasn't processing this yet."

Much like his daughter, Cassidy's father had fallen into a lake as a young boy. Being unable to swim, he too sank to the bottom. He began seeing a wave of colors while down there and heard a music he described to Cassidy's mother as the most beautiful music ever.

This left the young girl stunned, and Cassidy says the similarities between what she experienced, and what her dad experienced, are too much to ignore.

Many years have passed since Cassidy's near-death experience and learning her father had a similar encounter. She now has a family of her own and works in the dental industry. Since that fateful day, Cassidy has not been afraid of death because she's convinced she touched the other side while floating at the bottom of Cultus Lake.

She's also not forgotten the music she heard while down there. The colors she can sometimes attribute to a lack of oxygen to the brain, but the music, that feels like it was something else, says Cassidy.

"I can't even describe it, and I have a hard time believing my brain made that," she says.

"I really feel like there's so much more out there on another level that a lot of us don't realize and I really think something big was about to happen other than me dying."

A thirst for answers led Cassidy to the field of paranormal investigation, and she now spends her free time investigating alleged hauntings and spirit activity in Vancouver.

The experiences we've discussed so far all involve another presence being with the experiencer, be it being of light, a mysterious figure, or even a deceased family member. Cassidy's is different in that there was only the rainbow wave of colors coming toward her. She isn't sure what it was, and wonders if a being would have materialized had she not been pulled from the water.

"The music is what made me stop. The music was so riveting, and it was just so calming," she says.

What was that music? The calming effect is certainly in line with what other experiencers have discussed, but

Cassidy's is the first encounter Peter and I heard that involved music of any kind.

Cassidy mentions a social media video she watched where a musician connects plants and other organics to an electrical device and speaker. When a current is run from the device through the organics, they create a music that is quite similar to what she heard that day.

Peter has also witnessed similar experiments being conducted in the United Kingdom, saying the sounds created by connecting to plants and vegetation broadcast much like music.

Indeed, the Earth itself broadcasts at a frequency that's been dubbed the Schumann Resonance. Less like music and more like a steady, throbbing hum, this sound is used by monks and other meditation practitioners as part of grounding exercises. The Schumann Resonance is quite calming when listened to.

Unlike many experiencers, Cassidy hasn't found herself more empathic or possessing any kind of psychic abilities, she says. But she believes one hundred percent that we go somewhere else when we die.

"You're going somewhere. You're meeting somebody," she says.

And there's that interest in the paranormal as well. Cassidy relishes the opportunity to communicate with those who have already crossed over onto the other side.

"To have two parallel universes touch for a moment like a time burrito is an amazing experience," says Cassidy.

She's also found her experience and the personal knowledge of life after death has made it easier for her to weather the deaths of friends and relatives, and make those sad occasions into something more positive. Cassidy says there's an emotional sense of acceptance now, other than paralyzing grief.

Even looking back to the day she drowned, there's a part of her that felt sad to be lying on that dock instead of going wherever the rainbow wave and music intended to take her, she says.

"If someone were to say to me 'Marlene, you're going to die tomorrow,' I'd go and jump in the water," says Cassidy.

"It was so profoundly beautiful and peaceful."

Once again, a profound and peaceful experience one never forgets. It makes me wonder why our Western culture is so deathly afraid of, well, death? Especially when every person who has a near-death experience ceases to be afraid of dying and, in many cases, welcomes it when the time comes.

The same can be said for those of us who take up investigating the paranormal. The more encounters we have with the other side, whatever it may be, the more assured we become that something profound happens after we leave our physical body, and the less afraid – and more accepting – of that time we become.

Which brings us to an important question: what happens when we're on the other side? Do we stay one with some Divine entity? Or do we jump into another plane of existence, or even take on another life?

Let's talk with a couple who believe they've shared many lives together through the ages, and claim to be living proof of reincarnation.

CHAPTER TWELVE_
ALL OUR PASTS RELIVED

As we've heard already, people in a meditative state at times believe they've been able to journey to another plane of existence, and many are convinced this place they travel to is where we go when we die.

When David Bettenhausen meditated in 2014, he believes this deep, meditative state took him back to a life he once lived – and shared – with friend Carla Bogni-Kidd.

At first, he was taken back to an event that occurred in his current life on a beach in Boston in 1962. He was three years old and his father took the family to Boston because he was in grad school at the time.

Bettenhausen vividly recalled running on the beach, a giant Ferris wheel and rollercoaster from a nearby amusement park in the background. He was screaming with joy and a little girl in a blue, two-piece ruffled bathing suit ran up to him, pushed him down, and gave him a kiss on the forehead.

The little girl jumped back up, and asked the young Bettenhausen to be quiet, as his screaming was bothering her family. She then turned and ran off.

Startled by this memory, which he hadn't thought about since that day many decades earlier, he told Bogni-Kidd about it after meditation. Her response startled them both.

"That was me!" she said.

Both were godsmacked. To have briefly crossed paths twenty-six years before meeting again in 1998, and to not remember until now, felt like more than a coincidence. So they continued to meditate.

Eventually, Bettenhausen was struck by a vision that felt like another memory. This time he was standing in a dark alley looking at a woman. He knows this woman is Bogni-Kidd from the eyes and blonde hair, despite being younger than when they'd met in the present.

"She has this gold band on her head, slicked back blonde hair, and a fringed dress," he says.

Then his vision is filled with two quick flashes, and there's a pain in his chest. He's been shot! This shocks Bettenhausen from his meditation.

Undeterred, he decides to meditate again the next day. For whatever reason, Bettenhausen is sure he's onto something and determined to find answers to what feels like a very real memory, especially given the pain he felt in his chest the day before.

What happened next was like a memory bank download. Bettenhausen remembered seeing this woman, whom he believed to be Bogni-Kidd, at a wedding he'd been invited to. The wedding was for a man named Angelo, and the woman was a singer at the wedding. He and Bogni-Kidd hit it off at the reception, and he asked her out for breakfast. She accepted, and after breakfast, they went for a walk. Around them was the Chicago skyline.

During the walk, the woman told him her life story. She's from Bullock, Georgia, her name is Ruby Donaldson, and her father's name is James. She moved to Chicago to become a dress maker and a singer, and she worked at Andre's Speakeasy as a singer for a man named Angelo, who was a mobster.

The wedding they'd attended the night before took place on January 10, 1925!

"So I'm telling Carla this, all of this memory, how we became involved, and Carla jumps up and runs out of the room to do an investigation into all this," says Bettenhausen.

Bogni-Kidd says she wanted proof that her friend wasn't concocting a story while in a deep, meditative state. One of the sources she turned to was Ancestory.com, and sure enough, she found a Ruby Donaldson, born in Bullock, Georgia, in 1904. Using pictures and birth certificates, Bogni-Kidd was able to corroborate Donaldson's parents and ten other siblings.

"I also found a newspaper clipping for the wedding of Angelo Genna on January 10, 1925," she says.

Angelo "Bloody Angelo" Genna was an Italian-born bootlegger and organized crime leader during the Prohibition era in Chicago. He did indeed get married on January 10, 1925, to a Lucille Spingola and was killed after being shot several times during a high-speed car chase on May 26, 1925.

Bogni-Kidd found clippings and newspaper articles of the wedding, which was attended by some three thousand gangsters. She says she had no idea who Genna was before hearing Bettenhausen's story and digging into Ruby Donaldson.

"I called Dave and said 'You're not crazy. Guess what I found?'" she says.

"It's all true."

So Bettenhausen had a memory from his life that he couldn't remember, and a memory of a life during the roaring `20s from before he and Bogni-Kidd were born. A medical physician, Bettenhausen felt he'd lost his mind, he says.

This led Bettenhausen and Bogni-Kidd on a journey that ended in training alongside Dr. Brian Weiss, a psychiatrist and best-selling author who practices past-life regression. Their intention was never to perform past-life regression, but to meet others who'd had similar expe-riences.

Although he likes past-life regression as an experience, as a scientific method it is highly suggestible, says Bettenhausen.

"I don't know if you could use it as evidence of past lives," he says. "But so many people have this experience that I think it's at least interesting."

The quest for answers didn't end with Weiss and his past-life regression training. Bettenhausen and Bogni-Kidd continued to do research and dig deep into the reincarna-tion phenomenon.

Their research had them explore some two thousand five hundred accounts, including children who'd had spon-taneous memories of past lives. Some of these children were as young as three years old, says Bettenhausen. There was enough information included in these accounts that Department of Perceptual Studies professors considered it verified.

This is determined through a rigid process of inter-viewing the experiencer about his or her memories then going to great lengths to find the person they claimed to be in the past through historical research. This includes going over autopsy reports and tracking down homes identified in these memories. He says this information is brought back to the experiencer for further study. Sometimes they will pick the exact home they lived in out of a group of pictures, or identify a wound a body suffered from an autopsy report.

"They have a whole set of questions, and the kids, if they get the answers at least eighty percent correct – which is way better than their natural chance – they consider these kids are having some sort of verifiable memory," Bettenhausen says.

"Then they study personalities, they study birth marks because some times (the birth mark) follows them into another life. And if they get enough criteria, they document that case and publish it."

Bettenhausen believes these studies are proof something exists from life to life. Looking at scientific evidence of this phenomenon, he believes theories about consciousness are just that, theories, and explanations about consciousness vary from theory to theory.

However, there are cases where a patient suffers some form of brain damage and should not be able to recall certain memories, yet they still can. Bettenhausen says this creates an argument that memory and consciousness potentially exist somewhere outside the human brain and body.

If you're on board with the work of Bettenhausen and Bogni-Kidd, some thirty-three percent of the world's population believes in reincarnation, and twenty percent of Christians believe the same. They went as far as studying other religions – both were raised Catholic but are no longer practicing – to see how these religions view the phenomenon.

Judaism and Hinduism have a close relationship between God and reincarnation. Bettenhausen and Bogni-Kidd believe they have the same, going so far as to say they've met spirit guides who claim to be their connection – a tether if you will – between their current lives and God.

Taking things a step further, they've looked at everything from out-of-body experiences to alien abductions. They have also studied near-death experiences and how those could relate to the subject of reincarnation. Bettenhausen says the descriptions alien abductees have of their abductors is similar to those of spirit guides and even the beings of light described in near-death experiences.

These mysterious beings, the past-life review Panagore and Taylor mentioned, the tunnel of light, the loss of relevance of time, the sensation of moving quickly through space – all these things exist in most people's reincarnation memories, most near-death and abduction experiences, and even in cases of astral projection, says Bettenhausen.

"We really believe that the UFO/abduction experience is really a spiritual experience," he says. "They're out of body, they're awake, and in most of the UFO experiences, people really don't have physical evidence of the abduction. They only have this mental memory of the abduction. So maybe it's a nonphysical abduction or experience?"

Bettenhausen and Bogni-Kidd believe abductees are not physically abducted, they only feel they have been due to fear of this unknown experience. Their soul is simply having an experience in the spirit world.

Although a bit off topic, abduction experiences and reincarnation experiences are also similar in that the experiencer needs some kind of trigger to recall what happened. A sense of déjà vu or meeting someone for the first time who seems familiar.

"Most people who have a reincarnation experience, at least to start with, have a relatively traumatic event in a past life that comes forward. That's their first memory that comes forward," says Bettenhausen.

"Well, most people having an NDE, when they have a memory when they wake up, it's because the event was traumatic. It's something that causes a chemical, or spiritual, event that heightens their awareness and connects them to a memory that some people don't have."

If trauma is the trigger, then why don't more reincarnation experiencers remember their past lives, especially if they ended so tragically? Bettenhausen believes psychology and the study of the conscious and subconscious could provide an answer.

He says these memories are likely stored subconsciously in order to protect the experiencer not only from the memory, but also from meeting the same fate he or she did in the past. He likens it to a child accidently touching a hot pot; the first time they touch it they get burned, but the memory is forever stored away in the back of the mind so he or she doesn't touch the pot again.

It's only when something happens in the current life to jog these memories into the conscious mind that they resurface, he says.

I asked Bettenhausen and Bogni-Kidd if these past-life memories are triggered in order for the experiencer to try to correct a mistake from the past life in the current one? This could be to prevent a repeat of tragic or traumatic event in the past, or make up for the ill treatment of someone you knew in the past life, but met again in this life.

Bettenhausen says yes. He and Bogni-Kidd learned through their experiences that karma, which many perceive as a form of spiritual punishment, is actually more of a second chance to atone for past sins, even sins of a past life.

"You make a poor choice in a past life, you may be put in a situation again to try to overcome that choice. In our experience, it's part of what we call divine mercy and divine justice. You may have to face what you did to someone else to learn compassion, or you may have to face the same choice you made in the past that was incorrect," he says.

"Instead of one life and then hell, as a church might teach, it's chance after chance because God is one hundred percent merciful, but he's also just, so you have to face the situation until you overcome adversity and those changes."

In order to avoid falling into such a karmic situation, Bettenhausen and Bogni-Kidd developed five simple rules, which are to live a life without conceit, selfishness, jealousy, and unforgiveness, and to make all choices out of love.

"When you do that, you overcome all karma, you've lived on each side of every experience," he says.

As an example, Bogni-Kidd says she's lived a black life fourteen times out of thirty-four past lives. Bettenhausen says he's been black sixteen out of forty-two past lives. They have lived twenty-nine past lives together.

"So who's the slow learner?" Bogni-Kidd jokes.

Bettenhausen agrees and laughs.

All kidding aside, Bogni-Kidd says not every new life is lived in order to correct mistakes made in the past. Some times you come back to assist someone else in your Soul Family, which is the group of people who normally reincarnate back with you. Sisters, neighbors, friends – they all come back over and over again, which explains why we're very familiar with certain people and why sometimes we meet people and have a negative response immediately.

There's two reasons we come back together, she says. There are family mates – those we work well with together, have been together with in the past, and loved each other – and karmic mates – whom we have something to overcome with.

"It's not a sin, it's not a crime, it's not a punishment," says Bogni-Kidd. "It's a chance to get it right because how else do you learn? Everybody learns through adversity."

So do people share a similar relationship with others from life to life, or do the relationships change to suit whatever lesson needs to be learned? In their past lives together, Bogni-Kidd and Bettenhausen were brother and sister, she says. Their names were Katie and Johnny, and they lived in Chicago. She was six years old and he was four when they were playing on a third-story balcony on Christmas Eve and fell to their deaths.

Bogni-Kidd has been Bettenhausen's mother in the past, as well as his lover and even his neighbor, she says.

"Let's say you were a son and you had an abusive mother," says Bogni-Kidd. "Perhaps you will come back in reverse roles because how else will you learn?"

She and Bettenhausen view reincarnation as a way of breaking a cycle of abuse, or correcting the mistakes of the past. They also see reincarnation and the near-death experience as being intertwined. The near-death experience is simply an experience that occurs between lives.

In fact, the many parallels that we've covered in this chapter can't be mere coincidence, says Bettenhausen.

I agree, taking it back to how most near-death experiences are subjective, yet there are so many commonalities between them that they can't be discounted.

Bettenhausen believes reincarnation has its subjective experiences as well. He says people can only communicate the experiences they have. When it comes to near-death experiences, he believes they are more telepathic experiences with sight and sound but no physical encounters.

This is the same with the past-life memories. Bettenhausen says these are experienced telepathically. In both reincarnation and near-death experiences, only the one having the experience can describe it.

Taking this one step further, how we communicate these experiences will affect how we communicate with each other one day when we all share a non-physical existence, says Bettenhausen.

"That means there is a purpose to actually being here, and that's to learn shared communication because we are having shared experiences," he says.

This, in a way, echoes Scott Taylor's beliefs that we are here on Earth to understand duality and differing experiences. Bettenhausen agrees, saying if you've never experienced not being one with something, how can you appreciate the experience when you do?

"That's the duality question," he says.

So even for reincarnation, there is an endgame where experiencers will end up one with a divine source. Prior to speaking with Bettenhausen and Bogni-Kidd, I wondered how reincarnation could be included in a book about death, but having spoken with them, it makes perfect sense to have included their work in this volume.

What reincarnation and the near-death experience can teach us is there's not only more to life than what we see on the physical world, but there's more of a point to it than growing up, finding a job, starting a family and growing old – which is all fine. The point is to live this life well and treat others equally so. Much as with Panagore's findings, the story of Bettenhausen and Bogni-Kidd is inspiring.

Taking it back to the topic of near-death experiences directly, we have the story of Dan Gagné next.

CHAPTER THIRTEEN_
STARTING OVER

THE CIRCUMSTANCES SURROUNDING HIS DEATH IN AN automobile accident are still very clear in Dan Gagné's mind, even though he was just a teenager at the time.

He was sixteen years old and living in Fort Saint John in rural British Columbia, Canada. The date was July 23, 1989, and he was travelling in a red four-door 1967 Plymouth Reliant. He was driving, and a friend sat in the passenger's seat.

The road went from pavement to gravel, and Gagné was an inexperienced driver and hit the gravel too fast. To top things off the Plymouth was old and didn't have very good brakes.

As a result, the car ended up in a roadside ditch. Gagné gunned the engine, hoping to force the car out of the ditch and back onto the road.

"When I came back onto the road, the car did a complete one-eighty and then flipped out," says Gagné.

Given the age of the car, the two teens had only waist seatbelts to wear, as the lap-and-shoulder belts didn't exist when the vehicle was made. Gagné remembers hanging upside down in the overturned vehicle and being in a daze.

He saw the windshield was smashed out and felt a pain in his back and waist, he says.

"Hey," Gagné said to his friend. "Are you okay? Are you able to help me?"

His friend was fine and slipped out of the car and made his way around the vehicle to the driver's side. The friend got the door open and unfastened Gagné's seatbelt, at which point Gagné passed out.

When Gagné woke up, he wasn't in a hospital bed. He was completely surrounded by a white light, which he equates to being in the clouds or standing in an illuminated mist with nothing else present.

"I didn't know what was happening. I didn't know where I was. I didn't know why I was where I was," says Gagné.

All Gagné could think to do was stand and look around. He didn't even speak. Despite the strangeness of his surroundings, he felt calm. Like he didn't have a care in the world, he says.

This continued for an unknown amount of time before he saw a bright light appear and, for some reason, felt compelled to walk toward it. As he drew closer to the light, a transparent human figure appeared, one that looked like the quintessential representation of Jesus Christ.

"If you were to look at a picture of a guy with a beard, long hair, and a robe, you'd say he looks like Jesus," says Gagné, who was raised Catholic. "That's what I was led to believe my whole life."

Surrounding this figure was a yellow aura. No words were spoken, but the figure extended a hand toward Gagné, and Gagné knew he was to take this figure's hand and follow it. In that moment, Gagné believed he was dead, but he wasn't ready to go.

"I froze," he says. "If I take this hand, I'm really, really gone, and there's no going back."

In his mind, he told the figure he couldn't go with him because, if he went, it would kill his mom, says Gagné. His mom could not live with the fact her youngest son had died in a car accident.

Gagné has an older brother and sister.

The figure answered Gagné in his mind, telling him staying behind meant he would suffer. He would be in a lot of pain and encounter many struggles.

"It's going to be bad for you," the voice in his head told him.

"I'm better off for it to be bad for me than to be bad for my mom," Gagné replied telepathically.

The next thing Gagné knew, he was awake and in the

back of an ambulance with a paramedic excitedly yelling that they had him back and that he was alive, he says. Gagné was then told in French that he was in an ambulance heading to the hospital and that he'd be okay.

It turns out Gagné's friend had run down the road to get help when a passing motorist stopped. A lady in that vehicle knew first aid and was able to get Gagné out of the Plymouth and tend to him until an ambulance arrived. Any attempts to elicit a response from him in English failed, so the paramedic, who was bilingual, spoke to Gagné in French, and that's when he woke up.

Why French? Like many Canadians, Gagné grew up in a home where both English and French were spoken. Given Fort Saint John is a small town, the paramedic knew of Gagné and that he spoke both languages. When English failed, the paramedic tried French. The paramedic credits the use of French with bringing Gagné back.

Gagné isn't sure how long he was gone for. To him, it felt like ten minutes, but he doesn't believe so. He says his heart didn't stop beating at first either. It was only when he was pulled from the vehicle that it did, and the passing motorist made efforts to resuscitate him.

To readers, the lack of a sense of time, the white light and almost heaven-like setting, and the figure speaking telepathically should be very familiar by now. Although less dramatic, for lack of a better word, than Taylor's or

Panagore's story, Gagné's account fits very much into what we've explored during the course of this book.

Gagné grew up Catholic, so he believed he was in the religious version of Heaven. To him, the figure he met with looked like Jesus Christ, which supports the subjective notion of near-death experiences.

As a boy, he never had a choice when it came to going to church, he says. He and his siblings went, and that was that. Gagné's father was bipolar and manic depressive, and misconstrued the stories and parables in the Bible. When the family prayed, they knelt on bricks and held their hands outstretched before them. They did the rosary and prayed daily, went to church every Sunday, and gave ten percent of everything the family made back to the church.

"Looking back, it was a bit extreme," says Gagné. "We also grew up on a farm, so for us to go into town and go to church, it was a break because we didn't have to work."

As a boy, he took the family's religious ways as a good thing, and he wasn't aware of his father's mental disorders. He took his dad's extreme views and stern way as how all dads were, he says.

"Knowing the Bible inside and out, understanding it and interpreting it in my own way, I think it had a huge influence on what I saw. If I was of a different religion, I think the light would have been something else," says Gagné.

"It could've been a girl. It could've been Buddha."

Looking back, Gagné is surprised by the aptitude he had at the time to know he was dead and had literally gone to the Heaven he'd been told so much about, yet he didn't want to cause his mother such grief.

"She didn't deserve to have one of her children die before her," he says.

If the being Gagné encountered was indeed Jesus Christ, at least according to his upbringing, then Gagné believes Christ understood the love Gagné had for his mother outweighed whatever physical pain he'd face when he woke up, and that was okay. The boy didn't need to continue on to the other side.

So what of the stories Taylor and Panagore told of a life review and the presence of other souls in this vast existence of peace and light? Gagné says it was just the two of them, so if such a place exists, he simply hadn't got that far. Had he taken the figure's hand, he could very well have experienced all of that.

As in every other case, Gagné's life took a complete one eighty following his near-death experience, he says. Gagné was a bright kid, getting straight As in school simply by showing up. He didn't even have to study, retaining everything he read and heard. This wasn't the case with his siblings, as Gagné's sister was four years his senior, and he helped her with her homework.

The accident changed that. Gagné fractured the base of his skull and his left scapula, causing his head to swell up. He also fractured his spine and spent ten days in the hospital. To this day, he cannot lift the same amount with his left arm as he can with his right.

"I actually need help doing over-head stuff with my left arm," says Gagné. "So (the accident) impacted me physically."

The crash occurred during the summer between his eleventh and twelfth years in school. When he started grade 12, Gagné thought everything was back to normal, he says. But he quickly learned that he couldn't retain information the same as before.

Teachers would lecture, but Gagné couldn't grasp what they were saying. Gagné says he had to read everything three times in order to understand the material and retain it. His grades went from straight As to Cs and C pluses.

"And to me, being an over achiever, that was a failure," he says.

Doctors recommended Gagné travel from Fort Saint John to Vancouver to see a psychiatrist, and it was determined he'd suffered brain damage during the accident. In order to retain information, he was told to read everything three times, and not just read it, but speak it out loud or even act it out.

"Do the whole audible learning versus visual learning thing," says Gagné.

Gagné also developed a speech impediment, so he had

JASON HEWLETT & PETER RENN

to overcome that as well, he says. Even now, as he approaches fifty years of age, Gagné has to pause and think before he speaks because the words don't come to him as quickly as they should.

This is quite a different outcome than most of the other stories we've heard. Gagné's is the first near-death experience where we've learned of any physical impact, whereas others have talked about a grand spiritual awakening. So far, this has not been the case with his experience.

How about world view, or view of death? Gagné says he was young enough at the time of his accident where he hadn't contemplated his mortality much at all. Nor did he ever take stupid risks to tempt fate while growing up.

But he knows what is on the other side now, he says. If he dies before his time, or when he dies of old age, he's not afraid of that day coming, which is the exact position every near-death experiencer we interviewed found himself or herself in.

When it comes to developing any empathic or psychic abilities as a result of his experience, Gagné isn't sure. He's had moments where he's sensed some... thing around him, but he's doesn't know what that means.

Gagné couldn't sense this alleged spirit's presence at all, if it was even there, so he doesn't believe he came out of his experience with any real abilities of that nature, he says.

"I can't say I've ever had a paranormal experience since the accident," says Gagné.

That being said, he would like to join a group on a ghost hunting adventure simply to see if it's possible that he could have such an experience, he says.

"I'm definitely curious."

He's also unsure if he's inherited the empathic abilities others in this book have mentioned. However, he and his current wife did visit Salem, Massachusetts, where several locals were executed during the witch trials of 1692. Gagné says he and his wife were on a tour and came near the site where several hangings took place. Some sixth sense definitely let him know bad things had happened there. Whether or not that was a coincidence though, he's not sure.

Gagné has felt uneasy in the presence of people performing tarot-card readings, he says. He wonders if the feeling was a result of being around people who were totally open to the experience while he was closed to it.

"I just wanted to get out of there. I just felt so uncomfortable," he says. "As soon as I walked outside, I was fine."

Was something legitimately going on in the tarot room? Was Gagné being empathetic to the people in the room? He is unsure to this day.

Both Peter and I have had similar experiences to what Gagné just described. In fact, next time you go into a room, see if you can gauge the mood of the people in the room or see if you can pick up on how people feel when you are introduced to them. Their feelings are often projected into the environment around them, and you can "feel" if they are happy, angry, or sad. A lot of the time people sense this, but are not aware of what they are doing.

This ability can be learned and practiced whether someone has a near-death experience or not. As with anything else, it just takes practice.

We have two more near-death experiencers to introduce you to, and I want to continue with a similarly grounded story about a man named Jeff Hout from Surrey, British Columbia, before we venture across the pond to a more elaborate tale.

CHAPTER FOURTEEN_

MATTERS OF THE HEART

As an active sixty-two-year-old man, Jeff Hout likes to think cheating death is his thing. He beat colon cancer two years ago, which is no mean feat at any age, plus survived a bout of the COVID-19 pandemic.

He's run employment workshops for more than twenty-five years and coached youth football for forty years. He can still keep up with people a third of his age.

His near-death experience started about three months before he died, says Hout. At first, he thought he had the flu, which went away as all flus do, but he continued to get equally as sick once a month, which was unusual for him.

The third time the flu hit him it was accompanied by an intense headache that prevented him from getting any sleep. Frustrated, Hout decided to go to the hospital. This was late at night on a Friday, and he didn't want to trouble his wife by asking her to drive him, so he elected to drive himself.

Hout made it to the hospital and was examined by doctors. By then the pain in his head had worked its way down through his jaw and into his chest, and the doctors knew exactly what was going on.

"So basically what happened was I had a heart attack and I drove myself to the hospital," says Hout.

"Not a smart thing to do, apparently."

At the time, Hout shrugged his heart attack off. He was more concerned his parking ticket ran out at six in the morning, he says. The doctors told him he was going to be there for a while, so Hout phoned his wife and told her the bad news.

A couple of hours passed with Hout resting in a hospital bed. Then his condition took a turn for the worse. He says he was suddenly drenched in a cold sweat and felt nauseous. He also had trouble focusing, saying everything around him appeared to be in a fog.

"There were people moving around and talking, but I couldn't hear what they were saying," he says.

"Until I heard someone call for a crash cart."

A crash cart is a self-contained mobile unit that contains various medical supplies and medications designed for quick use in saving someone's life. As medical staff rushed toward him with a crash cart, he turned and looked at his heart monitor and watched it rapidly drop to flat line.

"And I said to myself, 'I'm going to go look for my dad; then I'm coming back,'" Hout says.

The next thing Hout knew, he was surrounded by light, a sensation he describes as the most beautiful experience he's ever had, much like the one many others in this book have talked about. Hout was pain free and at peace, the environment around him completely quiet.

"It was just beautiful," he says. "I don't know if I realized I was dead or not."

Reflecting back, Hout doesn't remember if he ventured through this realm or not. Nor is he sure of how long he was there. All he remembers is being surrounded by a bright, white light. Then there was a sudden shock, like he was slapped hard on the back of his left shoulder, and he woke up.

"I like to think it was my dad kicking me out and telling me it's not time yet," Hout says.

Hout had been resuscitated, and spent some time recovering his health in the hospital before being sent home. He later learned his wife was told the emergency room staff were barely able to bring him back to life. Hout never thought to ask how long he was gone for.

"It never seemed to matter to me, I guess," he says.

When pressed, Hout figures he was dead for less than a minute.

He had lingering effects from his near-death experience, which haunted him for a long time after. *Why am I here? Why did I come back?* Hout asked himself these questions all the time, essentially questioning his existence and his purpose in life. He even told his wife on at least one occasion he wished he hadn't come back, he says. These questions preceded a bout of mental health problems.

About two months after his experience, Hout stood on a local field, refereeing a football game. In hindsight he believes he should have taken the season off, but he wanted some normalcy in his life. However, it didn't take long before his thoughts started to race uncontrollably, and he felt he just shouldn't be there.

He collapsed onto one knee and began to hyperventilate, he says. With no idea what was happening to him or why, he started wailing.

"I was having a panic attack. I just didn't know it. I'd never had one before," says Hout.

These panic attacks continued from time to time, accompanied by prolonged periods of anxiety and depression, he says. Hout started meeting with a counsellor, which helped a bit but didn't bring an end to his woes. Soon he was plagued by suicidal thoughts.

This continued for three long and frustrating years with seemingly no end in sight. Then, while eating a meal together, Hout's wife choked on a piece of meat. Unable to breathe, she panicked, and her husband sprang into action.

Hout had first-aid training and was able to dislodge the meat from his wife's throat and clear the airway. After that, Hout's bouts with anxiety, depression and suicidal thoughts came to an end.

"If this is the only reason I came back, I'm okay with it," he says. "I was at peace at that point, and I haven't had those kinds of thoughts since then."

His work has helped a lot of people, and clients have even told Hout he's changed their lives. But, following his near-death experience, that didn't feel like enough, he says. To have experienced such exquisite peace and content-ment, there had to be more to being back than that. Saving his wife's life felt like the point to him being alive was made.

Hout credits his wife with helping him through those rough months and then years following his experience. He feels bad for putting her through it, but doesn't believe he would have made it without her support and understand-ing, he says.

"She's just the love of my life, and I would do anything for her," says Hout.

Prior to his near-death experience, Hout found himself very much in tune with other people and their moods, which helped him in his work and refereeing football. He believes the experience enhanced that empathic ability a bit.

For six and a half years Hout counselled addicts at a drug and alcohol treatment center, many of whom died multiple times as a result of their addictions. He says most never remembered their experiences due to how sick they were, but he'd share his personal brush with death with them. Hearing what Hout endured seemed to help them in their recovery.

"That's what people would tell me, and everybody would thank me for sharing that story with them," says Hout.

"I'm probably a little more empathetic than I was before."

Like everyone else we spoke to during the writing of this book, Hout isn't afraid of death. He's not sure he ever was, but now he's definitely ready for the day when it comes and is willing to step over to the other side with no regrets.

Which leaves us with one final story to share, one more in line with the experiences shared by Panagore and Taylor than Hout and Gagne.

CHAPTER FIFTEEN_
THE POINT OF IT ALL

FOR OUR FINAL CASE STUDY, WE PRESENT THE STORY of Mary Helen Hensley, who died on December 14, 1991. Reflecting back, her whole life up to that point was moving toward the moment of her death, because she wasn't using the unique abilities she'd been born with.

Her near-death experience was a wake-up call to her life's true purpose, she says.

"More or less, that accident happened in order to kind of reset my life, to give me an option out, or to give me an opportunity to change direction," says Hensley.

She was twenty-one years old when the accident happened and fresh out of college. Hensley had just moved to Charleston, South Carolina, the home of her college sweetheart, and despite studying for a career in marketing and design, she was mopping floors in a local sign shop, when the fateful day arrived.

In addition to not pursuing the career path she'd intended, Hensley says she believes she was also supposed to have followed a more spiritual path. The daughter of a minister, her mother fell ill with German measles while pregnant with her, and Hensley wasn't expected to live.

However, a group of celestial beings appeared before Hensley's father, and despite not understanding such things, her dad later told her the beings said she would survive and be endowed with gifts and abilities others didn't have, she says.

"You can imagine how completely out of his realm that was," says Hensley.

Sure enough, Hensley was born healthy and happy. By the time she turned four, her parents realized their little girl was talking with beings they couldn't see. In fact, she was communicating with the dead, including a grandfather who'd died when she was one year old.

"Then I was having dreams, and my dreams were coming true," she says. "Too much so to be coincidental."

Fearing their daughter would be exploited, her parents "put a lid" on her abilities. Hensley says she could talk about it with them all she liked, but not with anyone else. By the time she reached college, her ability, which she once believed would help her serve humanity in some way, was relegated to drinking games and predicting the scores for basketball games.

For Hensley, the car accident that killed her was a

course correction, intent on setting her on the path of helping others with her metaphysical healing abilities. It's also one she remembers vividly.

She was driving to a Christmas party on a very hot day, dressed in shorts and a T-shirt and a jingle bell... just to be festive. Her vehicle was on a side road heading onto a major highway and had stopped for a red light.

The light turned green, and Hensley crossed a couple of lanes of oncoming traffic in order to make a turn. She was driving across the last lane of traffic when she realized the driver speeding toward her wasn't going to stop.

"They estimated he was moving at seventy-five miles an hour when he ran through the red light," says Hensley.

Looking back, Hensley remembers everything slowing down at this point. She knew she was about to die and was given the choice to be inside her body, or out of it, when the moment happened, she says. She also had the very distinct feeling she'd lived this "moment of death," many times before.

"Everything was very familiar. It was not scary. I knew I could not stop it from happening," she says.

She decided to leave her body and watch the collision occur. Out of all the people we talked to, Hensley is the only one to describe such a near-death experience. She says there was a sound – a frequency – she heard the moment she left her body. This continued as a low tone for the duration of the collision, and Hensley equates it with keeping her connected to the Earth in order to witness her death.

As soon as she was above the highway, the scene sped up again, she says. She watched the vehicle collide with hers and her head smash into the driver's side window, breaking her neck. Her driver's seat folded up under her, and all the glass in the vehicle exploded outwards. Her car spun like a top across the road.

All of this she watched with the interest of a spectator at a sports game, she says. There were no tears or a pleading that she'd been taken too soon.

"It was just matter of fact," says Hensley.

She watched people gather to help, and could even feel what one spectator, a college friend, who happened to be a few cars behind her, felt as the tragedy unfolded and she realized who was in the car, Hensley says.

The sound changed from a low 'bagpipe' drone to something Hensley best describes as a celestial symphony, not unlike what Cassidy heard while under-water. Then everything sped up as Hensley believes she became that sound, that symphony, and was taken some-place else.

Hensley believes we, as people, are all frequencies and light, which is why some near-death experiencers see a tunnel of light and hers was a tunnel of sound, for lack of a better word.

The next place she inhabited was perfection, she says.

Hensley was completely at home and felt like she could stay there forever, but knew she had other places to go.

"It's like when you're on the best vacation ever and you're thinking 'Oh God, I don't want to go home,'" says Hensley. "Then all of a sudden you realize, 'I have stuff at home I really like.'"

This space Hensley found herself in was the transition spot between the living and the other side, she says. How long she was there for, she isn't sure. Eventually, an atmosphere formed around her – an atmosphere she also felt a part of. At the same time, she was very aware of who she'd just been in the physical world. As with other experiencers we've spoken with, Hensley knew she was an individual, but also felt connected to everything.

She also had a sense this wasn't the first time she'd been in this space, and knew instantly she'd lived many lives before. Hensley says she felt complete peace at this realization.

However, this was as far as Hensley, and any other near-death experiencer, would go. To go any further meant there would be no coming back, she says. This is the space between lives Bettenhausen and Bogni-Kidd described in an earlier chapter.

Still, she had no sense of panic or a desire to come back to life, so to speak. Hensley felt like she'd put in a good day's work, had shrugged off her work clothes, and was having a nice, cleansing shower.

"As I sat in that space, and you can sit in it as long as you need to, it started taking shape," she says. "Two beings stepped out of it. The atmosphere just became them and they came as very elderly men."

Hensley loves old people very much, enjoying their stories and spending time with them. She believes this is why the beings she saw were elderly. She says the men sat and waited with her until she realized these were her guardians and guides, who have been with her since the dawn of time.

There is a belief among many spiritual people that they aren't alone on their journey through life, or lives, depending on your belief system. These guides give you nudges along the way and even provide insight into how best to proceed in life.

Once Hensley clued in, her concept of space and time imploded, she says. Everything around her became like a three-hundred-and-sixty-degree cinema – a far cry from what she'd been told the afterlife would be as a kid in Sunday school. Playing on these multitude of screens were memories from her life, all at the same time. She saw herself getting lost when she was five years old, getting her driver's license at sixteen, hugging her first dog at age eleven, and getting wasted at a college party and raped at seventeen.

This is very much like the life review Taylor spoke of,

only tweaked to keep with Hensley's subjective near-death experience.

All these images and memories played out at the same time, and none seemed more important than the other, says Hensley. In fact, some of the more minute details stood out the most.

"You're watching this review, not in a linear timeline, but a concurrent timeline," she says.

"Until you sit in that space and experience it, it's just mind blowing and nearly impossible to perceive."

She quickly became aware that she was the one judging her life, her guardians seated beside her. In fact, Hensley believes she created her whole life experience, once again supporting the theory these are all subjective encounters.

Viewing these memories, what seemed important in life – like shedding those extra ten pounds – didn't matter anymore. In fact, most of what she thought about and worried about in life didn't even register, she says. And the memories playing out around her weren't all her highest achievements. In fact, there were equally as many failures and faults displayed to her.

"You're judging and critiquing yourself like you're watching a performance," says Hensley. "There's no win or lose. You're going 'Oh, that was awesome,' 'That's amazing,' or 'That was sweet. Look at how that changed this person's day.' 'Ooh, I'd do that differently now'... It's that kind of thing."

The review over, Hensley knew she was going back to the land of the living, she says. And she knew she was going back to a smashed-up body. Life, at least for the next while, would not be easy. Life was going to be a challenge, but she didn't care. In fact, the more difficult, the better.

"Bring it," she says.

Some of the near-death experiencers we talked to did not want to come back. Hensley believes she knew she had work to do, gifts she was supposed to share with the world, and that her life was going to be more purposeful. This is likely why she was so willing to come back and struggle through a painful recovery after the accident.

"I could've stayed if I wanted to. That's the interesting thing," she says, adding there were also portals she could travel through to check out different possible lives, much like what Panagore and I discussed earlier.

Hensley did come back. She worked through her recovery, and her life changed direction. She set aside her previous job and took on a new purpose in life intent before helping others navigate theirs, using her gifts – which had changed as a result of the near-death experience – to do so.

She went to chiropractic school, lured by the mind-body-spirit nature of the practice. Hensley says you can't work on one aspect, say the physical body, without it impacting one's emotional and spiritual bodies as well, and vice versa.

Now practicing metaphysics and chiropractic in Ireland, Hensley has helped some one–hundred–and–fifty-thousand patients. She says she can tell if someone has cancer simply by looking at them or working on them with her hands. This is done by picking up on the body's vibrational frequency, which Hensley equates to down-loading files off a computer.

"It's so cool to come in and touch somebody, download their hard drive, see the 'mind-movies' of their past or concurrent lifetimes, and go 'Oh, this is why this is happening now,'" says Hensley.

Ultimately, Hensley believes she can use her hands to literally go in and alter somebody's state of being – say assisting the body in removing a cancer or HIV or other disease. In the beginning, she and her clients would be shocked when the ailment would sometimes come back.

That's when Hensley realized she needed to help her patients understand the "why," which brought about the illness in the first place, she says. Each ailment has its own unique frequency or sound, and all she needs to do is feel and hear it to know what it is. All it takes is a chemical reaction on the part of the patient to access a memory, face it, and reconcile what they did or what happened to them in order to clear the trauma and move forward.

Whew!

That's a lot, and one must admit, it does sound pretty unbelievable. But when you take into account a lot of what's been touched on in this book, Hensley's claims fit within the narrative, so far. Taylor and Bettenhausen and Bogni-Kidd spoke at length about vibrational frequencies and how tapping into those can literally put you in a different frame of mind, if not a different plane of existence, altogether. Bettenhausen and Bogni-Kidd spoke at length about past lives and correcting past mistakes in the present. Sound and music played a big role in Cassidy's near-death experience.

Could all this be connected in much the same way as many paranormal researchers believe all aspects of the paranormal, be they ghosts, unidentified flying objects, and beings like Mothman and Bigfoot, are all part of the same phenomenon? At first, the idea seems outlandish, but...

Hensley says it doesn't matter if it's a past life or present one, it's all about people taking responsibility for their lives and their own health. Sadly, even when all the information one needs to correct issues of the mind, body and spirit, is placed in a patient's hands, they still often won't do what is necessary to improve their situation.

Why?

"Because we're inherently lazy," says Hensley. "We want someone to do it for us rather than take responsibility, because taking responsibility can potentially be so painful." I believe fear also plays a role in this.

Once you realize there's more to life than what most of us see on the surface, it's hard to unsee it. A person's perception of the world is forever changed. Some people literally talk themselves out of the experience so they can go back to living a simple life where they don't have to take responsibility for anything, and there are no consequences waiting for them.

The thing is, if you believe the stories you've read in this book, it doesn't matter what you believe: you will be held accountable for your actions in this life, and if you believe some of the experiences we've discussed, there will be consequences waiting for you on the other side, and possibly in the next life you live.

So the question I want to leave you with is a simple one: what do you believe?

ABOUT THE AUTHORS_

Jason Hewlett is a journalist, broadcaster, and podcaster with a degree in filmmaking and film studies. A lifelong interest in the paranormal led him to join Vancouver Paranormal Society in 2017, where he was a lead investigator and society director until 2020, when he and colleague Peter Renn launched the Canadian Paranormal Foundation. In 2021 Jason became the manager of The Paranormal Network, a YouTube channel dedicated to high strangeness. He is the writer, director and co-creator of the award-winning paranormal reality series We Want to Believe, narrator for The UFO Show, and co-host of Hunting the Haunted, all of which are on The Paranormal Network. In 2020, Jason and Peter co-authored the best-selling book I Want to Believe: One Man's Journey into the Paranormal, which highlights Peter's career as a paranormal investigator.

———

Peter Renn has more than 27-years-experience as a paranormal investigator. Born in London, England, he's been fortunate to investigate documented locations all around the world, and specializes in negative (demonic) cases. He's also a documenting investigator for an exorcist in Washington state. Skeptical by nature, Peter looks for a logical explanation first, before jumping to paranormal conclusions. Peter is an executive producer and the lead investigator for We Want to Believe, and co-host of Hunting the Haunted, which are broadcast on The Paranormal Network YouTube channel. He was director of Vancouver Paranormal Society for a decade, but left in 2020 to launch the Canadian Paranormal Foundation with Jason Hewlett.

I Want to Believe: One Man's Journey Into
The Paranormal

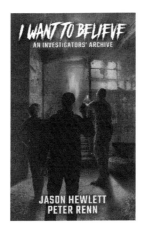

I Want to Believe: An Investigators' Archive